Teaching Systematic Synthetic Phonics: Audit and Test

Transforming Primary QTS

Teaching Systematic Synthetic Phonics: Audit and Test

David Waugh and Ruth Harrison-Palmer

Series editor: Alice Hansen

Los Angeles | London | New Delhi
Singapore | Washington DC

Learning Matters
An imprint of SAGE Publications Ltd
1 Oliver's Yard
55 City Road
London EC1Y 1SP

SAGE Publications Inc.
2455 Teller Road
Thousand Oaks, California 91320

SAGE Publications India Pvt Ltd
B 1/I 1 Mohan Cooperative Industrial Area
Mathura Road
New Delhi 110 044

SAGE Publications Asia-Pacific Pte Ltd
3 Church Street
#10-04 Samsung Hub
Singapore 049483

Editor: Amy Thornton
Development editor: Jennifer Clark
Production controller: Chris Marke
Project management: Deer Park Productions, Tavistock,
Devon, England
Marketing Manager: Catherine Slinn
Cover design: Wendy Scott
Typeset by: C&M Digitals (P) Ltd, Chennai, India
Printed and bound by Henry Ling Limited, at the Dorset
Press, Dorchester, DT1 1HD

Library of Congress Control Number: 2013946206

British Library Cataloguing in Publication data

A catalogue record for this book is available from the
British Library

MIX
Paper from
responsible sources
FSC® C013985
www.fsc.org

ISBN: 978-1-4462-6894-0
ISBN: 978-1-4462-6895-7 (pbk)

Contents

About the authors and series editor   vii

Introduction   ix

1.   Discriminating sounds and phonemes   1

2.   Challenges   6

3.   Grapheme–phoneme correspondences and
     'tricky words'   13

4.   Decoding and encoding text   19

5.   Long vowel digraphs   25

6.   Spelling   30

7.   Teaching phonics in the early years   39

8.   Multisensory approaches   45

9.   Teaching a systematic and structured programme   50

10. Planning for phonics   59

11.   Tracking and assessing pupils' learning   65

12.   Phonics at Key Stage 2   78

13.   Using a range of programmes and resources   89

Conclusion   97

Appendix 1: initial audit answers   99

Appendix 2: long audit   100

Appendix 3: long audit answers   112

Index   121

About the authors and series editor

The authors

David Waugh

David Waugh is Director of Primary PGCE at Durham University where he is also the subject leader for English. He has published extensively in Primary English. David is a former deputy head teacher, was Head of the Education Department at the University of Hull, and was Regional Adviser for ITT for the National Strategies from 2008 to 2010. As well as his educational writing, David also writes children's stories.

Ruth Harrison-Palmer

Ruth Harrison-Palmer is a former acting head teacher. She has worked for the National Strategies and Cumbria Local Authority as a literacy consultant. Currently Ruth has a senior role in ITE at the University of Cumbria.

The series editor

Alice Hansen

Alice Hansen is the Director of Children Count Ltd where she is an educational consultant. Her work includes running professional development courses and events for teachers and teacher trainers, research and publishing. Alice has worked in education in England and abroad. Prior to her current work she was a primary mathematics tutor and the programme leader for a full-time primary PGCE programme at a large university in England.

Introduction

In England, the Teachers' Standards require that teachers 'demonstrate good subject and curriculum knowledge' and 'if teaching early reading, demonstrate a clear understanding of systematic synthetic phonics' (DfE, 2012: 7).

This book is designed to help you to identify aspects of systematic synthetic phonics which you already understand as well as those which you will need to explore further.

How to use this book

Each chapter asks you to define key terminology for an aspect of phonics teaching and learning. This is followed by a series of questions and activities. Each chapter also includes the answers (or in some cases, suggested answers) to the audits together with brief explanations. Although it can be used without it, the book is linked closely to another text: Jolliffe *et al.* (2012) *Teaching Systematic Synthetic Phonics in Primary Schools*. The chapters in the two books are matched, so that you can read about the aspects in the audits in more detail by reading Jolliffe *et al.*

At the end of the book, you will find a longer audit, which you should attempt once you have worked through the audits in the chapters. But first, try the initial audit below to see how much you know already and some of the things which you will need to find out more about.

Initial audit

You will find answers to the initial audit at the end of the book in Appendix 1.

What does word recognition refer to in the Simple View of Reading?
What does language comprehension refer to in the Simple View of Reading?
What is a phoneme?

What is a grapheme?
How many phonemes do you think there are in English?
What is blending?
What is segmenting?
How many vowel sounds do you think there are?
How many consonant sounds?
What is encoding?
What is decoding?
How many phonemes are there in each of these? cat book flat splash crack blend phonics

What else you need to do

At the end of each chapter you will find some suggested websites which will help you to find out more or will provide examples and activities. You will also find recommended reading and suggestions as to what you might do next to develop your understanding.

We hope you will find this book not only helps you to check on your knowledge and understanding of systematic synthetic phonics, but also provides a useful starting point for further exploration of this important aspect of primary education.

David Waugh

Ruth Harrison-Palmer

August 2013

References

DfE (2012, revised June 2013) *Teachers' Standards* (available at **https://www.gov.uk/ government/uploads/system/uploads/attachment_data/file/208682/Teachers__ Standards_2013.pdf**).

Jolliffe, W. and Waugh, D. with Carss, A. (2012) *Teaching Systematic Synthetic Phonics in Primary Schools*. London: Learning Matters/SAGE.

1 Discriminating sounds and phonemes

Work through each section below, responding to each question or task. When you have completed each section, you can read the answers at the end of the chapter. At the end of this chapter you can also find support for further reading and study related to discriminating sounds and phonemes.

Section 1: key terminology for discriminating sounds and phonemes

It is important that you understand the terms below before you move on to the next activity. Provide a definition of each and check your definitions against those given later in this chapter:

- phonemes

- graphemes

- phonological awareness

- phonemic awareness

- segmentation and blending

- adjacent consonants

Section 2: segmenting words

Test your knowledge by trying to work out the number of phonemes in the words below. Remember that there are always the same number of phonemes as graphemes, as a grapheme can be any number of letters that represent that phoneme.

Remember:

- in 'bat' we can hear 3 phonemes: b/ a/ t/
- in 'ship' we can hear 3 phonemes: sh/ i/ p/
- In 'night' we can hear 3 phonemes: n/ igh/ t/

Word	Number of phonemes	Split the word into phonemes	Word	Number of phonemes	Split the word into phonemes
then	3	/th/e/n/	stress		
chip			strap		
bring			flow		
crash			brand		
way			bake		

Section 3: phoneme frames

In schools, many teachers use phoneme frames to help children to segment words into phonemes and graphemes. For example:

sh	a	n	d	y	
b	r	igh	t		
f	l	a	sh	i	ng

Use the frame below to segment the following words: *blow, shortly, blast, window, draining*:

Answers

Section 1: key terminology for discriminating sounds and phonemes

Phonemes
Phonemes are individual sounds. In English, there are around 44 phonemes (the number varies slightly according to accent and which phonics programme you look at).

Graphemes

Graphemes are phonemes written down, so in the word *cat* there are three phonemes and they are represented by three graphemes /c/a/t/. In the word *shop* there are three phonemes but the first is represented by two letters making one sound (a digraph):/sh/o/p/.

Phonological awareness

Phonological awareness involves being able to hear, recall and manipulate sounds.

Phonemic awareness

Phonemic awareness is the ability to hear and manipulate the phonemes in spoken words and to remember the order of phonemes in words. For example, the phonemes in the word *big* can be segmented as /b/ /i/ /g/.

Segmentation and blending

Oral blending and segmentation, which are the reverse of each other, help children to blend and segment for reading and spelling when they learn letters and sounds.

Adjacent consonants

Consonants which are side by side but have separate phonemes – for example, s/t in *stop*, c/l in *club* and s/t/r in *strip*. Although we blend these sounds together, it is important to emphasise that the letters each have individual sounds.

Section 2: segmenting words

Word	Number of phonemes	Split the word into phonemes	Word	Number of phonemes	Split the word into phonemes
then	3	/th/e/n/	stress	4	/s/t/r/e/ss/
chip	3	/ch/i/p/	strap	5	/s/t/r/a/p/
bring	4	/b/r/i/ng/	flow	3	/f/l/ow/
crash	4	/c/r/a/sh/	brand	5	/b/r/a/n/d/
way	2	/w/ay/	bake	3	/b/a/k/e

If you managed to segment all the words correctly, well done! If you didn't you may have struggled because you are already a sophisticated reader who doesn't always pay attention to every sound in a word. For example, you may have segmented *stress* as str/e/ss/ because you are used to seeing *str* in words and assume that this is a single sound. In fact, *str* is three sounds. Try saying the letter sounds slowly and notice what happens in your mouth: you make three different shapes – one for each letter sound or phoneme.

You may similarly have decided that *crash* should be segmented as cr/a/sh/ because you are familiar with words which begin with *cr* (*crack*, *crumb*, *cricket*). Again, try sounding the phonemes slowly and you will notice that your mouth makes two shapes as you do so. These groups of letters which occur frequently in words are called consonant clusters or consonant blends and more recently adjacent consonants. It is very useful for readers to be aware of them as their reading develops, but beginner readers need to be able to identify every sound in new words if they are to be able to say them correctly and then spell them accurately.

Section 3: phoneme frames

b	l	ow			
sh	or	t	l	y	
b	l	a	s	t	
w	i	n	d	ow	
d	r	ai	n	i	ng

How did you manage this time? In the first word, *blow*, there are three phonemes and you needed not only to realise that *bl* represents two sounds, but also that *ow* represents a single sound which is represented by two letters: a digraph. Try saying *ow*, making the same sound as in *blow*. Notice that your mouth stays open throughout, which is a feature of vowel phonemes:

- In *shortly*, *sh* represents a single sound and both letters are consonants, so *sh* is a **consonant digraph**. The *or* part of the word is a single sound and even though *r* is a consonant the sound is a vowel sound, so *or* is referred to as a **vowel digraph**.

- *Blast* has five sounds, although the *bl* at the beginning and *st* at the end are consonant clusters, but each represents two sounds.

- *Window* has a vowel digraph at the end (*ow*) – notice that your mouth remains open as you make the sound.

- *Draining* includes the vowel digraph *ai*, which you probably spotted, but did you decide that the *ng* at the end was one sound or two? For most English-speakers *ng* is a single sound, but for some, particularly in parts of the English Midlands and some areas in Yorkshire, *ng* can be sounded as two sounds. Phonics programmes tend to regard *ng* as a single sound.

The split vowel digraph

In Chapter 5 you will look at words in which the vowel sound is made by two letters which are not immediately adjacent to each other (as in *make, safe, bite* etc.).

What to do next?

Reinforce your knowledge and understanding of segmenting by doing as many as possible of the following:

- Observe teachers working with children and note how they model segmenting. How do they show children how to count phonemes?

- Read Chapter 1 in *Teaching Systematic Synthetic Phonics in Primary Schools* (Jolliffe *et al.*, 2012) to find out more about blending and segmenting.

- Practise with a colleague segmenting the following words. The number of phonemes for each is given in brackets. Decide between you how to segment each word into its individual sounds: *smash* (4), *dart* (3), *grab* (4), *chocolate* (7), *bean* (3), *Sunday* (5).

Websites

There are several useful websites where you can find examples of blending and segmenting and watch videos of teachers at work. These include:

Mr Thorne Does Phonics (**http://www.youtube.com/watch?v=hm4nhA4b-2Q**).

Recommended reading

DCSF (2007) *Letters and Sounds: principles and practice of high quality phonics*. London: DCSF.

DCSF (2009) *Support for Spelling*. London: DCSF.

Johnston, R. and Watson, J. (2007) *Teaching Synthetic Phonics*. Exeter: Learning Matters/ SAGE.

Jolliffe, W. (2006) *Phonics: a complete synthetic programme*. Leamington Spa: Scholastic.

Jolliffe, W. (2007) *You Can Teach Synthetic Phonics*. Leamington Spa: Scholastic.

Jolliffe, W. and Waugh, D. with Carss, A. (2012) *Teaching Systematic Synthetic Phonics in Primary Schools*. London: Learning Matters/SAGE (Chapter 1).

2 Challenges

Learning outcomes

This chapter will help you to audit your:

- understanding of the importance of correct enunciation of phonemes;
- understanding of issues related to accent;
- understanding of phoneme and grapheme variations;
- knowledge of strategies to help parents to support their children's reading effectively.

Work through each section below, responding to each question or task. When you have completed each section, you can read the answers at the end of the chapter. At the end of this chapter you can also find support for further reading and study related to the challenges of teaching systematic synthetic phonics.

Section 1: key terminology for challenges

It is important that you understand the terms below before you move on to the next activity. Provide a definition of each and check your definitions against those given later in this chapter:

- accent

- dialect

- schwa

- enunciation

- grapheme variation

- phoneme variation

Section 2: phonics problems

Look at each of the following and consider:

- why you think the problem arose;

- how you might address it.

1. A child in your Y2 class often writes *fink*, *fank* and *fort* etc for words beginning with a soft *th* like *think*, *thank* and *thought*.

2. Some children in your new Y3 class sound out words to spell them, but often add unnecessary letters. For example, there are spellings such as *duogu* for *dog* and *cuatu* for *cat*.

3. In your Y1 class several children add an unnecessary *i* to words like *sky* (*skiy*) and *why* (*wiy*).

4. You inherit a Y2 class from a teacher from London and find children adding unnecessary *r*s to some words such as *fast* (*farst*), *plastic* (*plarstic*) and *path* (*parth*).

5. A girl in your Y4 class spells *no* as *now*, *go* as *gow*, and *show* as *showa*.

6. A Y3 boy regularly confuses long vowel digraphs in simple words such as *rain* (*rane*, *rayn*), *blow* (*bloa*, *bloe*) and *team* (*teme*, *teem*).

Section 3: grapheme variations

Many phonemes can be represented by more than one grapheme. For example, the *k* sound at the beginning of *king* can be made by *ck* at the end of *kick*, *c* in *cat*, *cc* in *account*, *q* in *Iraq* and *ch* in *school*. Look at the graphemes below and see how many alternative ways each can be represented, providing a word for each example:

- the *sh* sound in *shop*
- the *f* sound in *fish*
- the *j* sound in *jug*
- the *n* sound in *not*
- the *ee* sound in *feet*
- the *ai* sound in *train*
- the *ou* sound in *loud*
- the *oo* sound in *food*
- the *o* sound in *no*
- the *schwa* sound in *the*

Section 4: phoneme variations

Just as different graphemes can represent the same sound, so many graphemes can be used for more than one phoneme. For example, *c* can be sounded differently in *cat* and *city*, *ch* can be sounded differently in *chip*, *chef* and *school*, and *o* is sounded differently in *no*, *not* and *woman*.

Look at the graphemes below and see how many alternative phonemes each can be used to represent, providing a word for each example:

- *f*

- *g*

- *s*

- *ou*

- *ea*

- *ow*

- *y*

- *ough*

- *th*

- *k*

Answers

Section 1: key terminology for challenges

It is important that you understand the terms below before you move on to the next activity.

Accent

A dialect can be spoken with different accents. Our accent is the way we pronounce words, whereas our dialect has a grammatical structure, even if this is not written down as with Standard English.

Dialect

All versions of a language are dialects and include words, phrases and clauses which may not appear in other dialects. Standard English is the dialect which is often accepted as 'correct' and is the version in which English should be written. It should not be confused with accent.

Schwa

A schwa is a short vowel sound such as we hear in words like *the*, *pencil*, *doctor* and *taken*. The symbol often used to show the schwa sound in dictionaries is Ə. Say each of those words and notice the short sound made by the letters in bold: the, pencil, doctor and taken.

Enunciation

This means to pronounce or articulate. It is important that we enunciate phonemes clearly and accurately when teaching children. This means avoiding adding additional sounds such as the schwa wherever possible. For many letters this is quite easy – for example, *f*, *l*, *m*, *n*, *r*, *s*. For some, however, it is difficult to avoid (*b*, *d*, *t*), but you should try to keep this as short as possible.

Grapheme variation

Many phonemes can be represented by different graphemes. For example, the *ie* sound in *tie* can be represented by *-igh* in *high*, *y* in *by*, and *eigh* in *height*.

Phoneme variation

Many graphemes can represent different phonemes. For example, *g* has different sounds in *gate*, *germ* and *regime*.

Section 2: phonics problems

Look at each of the following and consider:

- why you think the problem arose;

- how you might address it.

1. This problem is probably caused either by the child's inability to pronounce *th* correctly or by hearing an adult (perhaps a parent or even a teacher) mispronounce *th*. Focus on mouth shape when making the sound. There are many websites and a DVD which accompanies *Letters and Sounds* which show mouth actions as phonemes are enunciated.

2. This is probably caused by the children having been taught by someone who didn't enunciate correctly, adding a schwa sound to consonants, for example saying *suh* rather than *ss* for *s*. Work on correct enunciation for yourself and the children. Talk with parents about correct enunciation. Look at examples online and in the *Letters and Sounds* DVD.

3. This problem is probably caused by children's pronunciation and the fact that they 'hear' a *y* sound at the end of *why* and *sky* when some people say the words. This leads to them adding an extra letter. Try saying *sky* and *why* and notice what happens in your mouth: you can say the words keeping your mouth wide open at the end or you can bring your tongue up to your palate. If you do the latter you tend to add a slight additional sound. Work on correct enunciation for yourself and the children. Look at lots of examples of words which have *y* at the end making an *ie* sound, for example, *by*, *try*, *my*, *reply*, *fly*, and talk about how they are spelt.

4. This is probably caused by the children having assumed that there was an *r* in the words due to their previous teacher's pronunciation. Talk with the children about different accents – there will be several in the class. Play extracts from TV programmes or websites in which people speak with a range of accents. Emphasise that their teacher and others who use a long *a* in some words are not speaking incorrectly, just differently.

5. This problem is probably caused by the girl hearing a *w* sound when these words are spoken. Notice how your lips almost meet at the end of such words. Try saying *go away* and notice how you make a *w* sound between *go* and *away*. If children are used to hearing *w* enunciated with a pronounced *schwa* sound, they may assume that an additional letter is needed when spelling words like *flow* and *show*. Look at words which have a long *oe* sound at the end and discuss spellings. Focus, in particular, on those which end with *o* and *ow*.

6. On the whole these might be considered 'good' spelling mistakes, since they are phonically plausible. The errors probably arise due to a lack of familiarity with the words in print. Look at words with long vowel digraphs and discuss spellings. Through discussions and investigations, build sets of word families for long vowel phonemes – for example, *rain, pain, gain; seem, street, greet*. Talk about spellings which are likely and less likely – for example, words tend not to have *ay* as an *ay* sound except at the end.

Section 3: grapheme variations

You were asked to look at the graphemes below and see how many alternative ways each can be represented, providing a word for each example. Some possible answers are shown below. You may have thought of many others too.

1. The *sh* sound in *shop* – *ch* in *chef*, *ci* in *delicious*, *ti* in *nation*
2. The *f* sound in *fish* – *ph* in *photograph*, *gh* in *laugh*, *ff* in *off*
3. The *j* sound in *jug* – *g* in *gem*, *-dge* in *edge*
4. The *n* sound in *not* – *gn* in *gnat*, *kn* in *knit*, *pn* in *pneumatic*, *nn* in *dinner*
5. The *ee* sound in *feet* – *ea* in *read*, *ei* in *receive*, *ie* in *grief*, *e-e* in *eve*
6. The *ai* sound in *train* – *ay* in *day*, *eigh* in *weigh*, *ey* in *grey*
7. The *ou* sound in *loud* – *ow* in *now*, *ough* in *bough*
8. The *oo* sound in *food* – *ew* in *threw*, *ough* in *through*, *u-e* in *rude*
9. The *o* sound in *no* – *ow* in *know*, *oa* in *coat*, *o-e* in *nose*
10. The schwa sound in *the* – *a* in *woman*, *or* in *doctor*, *er* in *teacher*

Section 4: phoneme variations

You were asked to look at the graphemes and see how many alternative phonemes each can be used to represent, providing a word for each example. You can see some possibilities below, but you probably found more:

1. f: fat, of
2. g: get, germ, gnat

3. s: sit, is, sugar
4. ou: noun, tough, cough
5. ea: head, meat, steak, idea, earth
6. ow: now, know
7. y: you, by, easy
8. ough: tough, bough, bought, cough, through, though
9. th: this, think
10. k: kick, know

What to do next?

Reinforce your knowledge and understanding of segmenting by doing as many as possible of the following:

- Observe teachers working with children and note how they model segmenting. How do they show children how to count phonemes?

- Read Chapter 2 in *Teaching Systematic Synthetic Phonics in Primary Schools* (Jolliffe *et al.*, 2012) to find out more about some of the challenges we face when teaching phonics.

Websites

There are several useful websites where you can find examples of blending and segmenting and watch videos of teachers at work. These include:

Mr Thorne Does Phonics **www.mrthorne.com/**

Sonic Phonics (2011) Product available at **www.talkingproducts.com/sonic-phonics.html**.

Recommended reading

DCSF (2009) *Support for Spelling*. London: DCSF.

DfE (2011) *Teachers' Standards in England from September 2012*. London: Department for Education.

DfES (2007) *Letters and Sounds: principles and practice of high quality phonics*. London: DfES.

Get Reading Right (2012) *Pronouncing the Phonemes*. York: Get Reading Right. Available at **www.getreadingright.co.uk/phoneme/pronounce-the-phonemes**.

Johnston, R. and Watson, J. (2007) *Teaching Synthetic Phonics*. Exeter: Learning Matters/SAGE.

Jolliffe, W. (2006) *Phonics: a complete synthetic programme*. Leamington Spa: Scholastic.

Jolliffe, W. (2007) *You Can Teach Synthetic Phonics*. Leamington Spa: Scholastic.

Jolliffe, W. and Waugh, D. with Carss, A. (2012) *Teaching Systematic Synthetic Phonics in Primary Schools*. London: Learning Matters/SAGE (Chapter 2).

McGuinness, D. (2004) *Early Reading Instruction: what science really tells us about how to teach reading*. Cambridge, MA: MIT Press.

Miskin, R. (2006) *Read Write Inc. Phonics Handbook*. Oxford: Oxford University Press.

Ofsted (2011) *Getting Them Reading Early* (Ref: 110122). Available at **www.ofsted. gov.uk/resources/getting-them-reading-early**. Manchester: Ofsted.

3 Grapheme–phoneme correspondences and 'tricky words'

Learning outcomes

This chapter will help you to audit your:

- understanding of challenges presented by the English alphabetical system in which 44 sounds are represented by 26 letters and over 400 combinations of letters;
- ability to map 44 phonemes to 26 letters;
- understanding of strategies for teaching irregular and less common grapheme–phoneme correspondences.

Work through each section below, responding to each question or task. When you have completed each section, you can read the answers at the end of the chapter. At the end of the chapter, you can also find support for further reading and study related to tricky words.

Section 1: key terminology for grapheme–phoneme correspondences and 'tricky' words

It is important that you understand the terms below before you move on to the next activity. Provide a definition of each and check your definitions against those at the end of the chapter:

- orthographic system
- decodable
- decoding
- encoding
- phonically irregular
- mnemonic
- over-syllabification

Section 2: grapheme–phoneme correspondences – 'grotty graphemes'

The phonics programme Read Write Inc. uses the term 'grotty grapheme' for the graphemes which make a word 'tricky'. For example, in *said*, the *ai* in the middle is a short vowel sound rather than the long vowel sound usually made by *ai* (*rain*, *pain*, *drain* etc).

These 'grotty graphemes' become less of a challenge as children develop their knowledge of more complex grapheme–phoneme correspondences. For the purposes of this activity, we have used the grapheme–phoneme correspondences defined in *Letters and Sounds* phases two and three as follows:

Phase 2	Phase 3
Set 1: s, a, t, p	Set 6: j, v, w, x
Set 2: i, n, m, d	Set 7: y, z, zz, qu
Set 3: g, o, c, k	
Set 4: ck, e, u, r	
Set 5: h, b, f, ff, l, ll, ss	

Phase 3

Graphemes	Sample words	Graphemes	Sample words
ch	chip	ar	farm
sh	shop	or	for
th	thin/then	ur	hurt
ng	ring	ow	cow
ai	rain	oi	coin
ee	feet	ear	dear
igh	night	air	fair
oa	boat	ure	sure
oo	boot/look	er	corner

Based on knowledge of the grapheme–phoneme correspondences in phase two and three above, identify the 'grotty graphemes' in the following common words:

old	*was*	*have*	*no*	*he*	*you*
day	*saw*	*were*	*your*	*here*	*they*

Section 3: identifying tricky bits in the 50 most common English words

For children with knowledge of the grapheme–phoneme correspondence above, try to identify any tricky bits in the 50 most common words. Consider why they might be tricky. The first few have been done for you and are presented in underlined bold type. Not all the words contain tricky bits.

the	w**a**s	that	th**ere**	then
and	y**ou**	with	out	w**ere**
a	they	all	this	go
to	on	we	have	little
said	she	are	went	as
in	is	up	be	no
he	for	had	like	mum
I	at	my	some	one
of	his	her	so	do
it	but	what	not	me

Source: from Masterson, J., Stuart, M., Dixon, M. and Lovejoy, S. (2003) *Children's Printed Word Database*. Economic and Social Research Council funded project, R00023406.

Section 4: exploring alternative spellings

You will meet many spelling mistakes from your pupils. To understand why children spell as they do, it is useful to explore possible alternative, but incorrect, spellings for some common words, for example, *fish – phish*, *once – wons*, *tough – tuff*.

See how many phonically plausible different ways you could spell each of the following:

- *germ*
- *school*
- *make*
- *because*
- *could*
- *said*

Answers

Section 1: key terminology for grapheme–phoneme correspondences and 'tricky' words

Orthographic system
The spelling system of a language – i.e. the ways in which graphemes and phonemes relate to each other. The English orthographic system is more complex than many languages, since most phonemes can be represented by more than one grapheme.

Decodable
Words which can be easily decoded using phonic strategies, e.g. *cat*, *dog*, *lamp*.

Decoding
The act of translating graphemes into phonemes – i.e. reading.

Encoding
The act of transcribing units of sound or phonemes into graphemes – i.e. spelling.

Phonically irregular
Words that are not easily decoded because they do not conform to common grapheme–phoneme correspondences.

Mnemonic
A device for remembering something, such as 'ee/ee/ feel the tree'.

Section 2: grapheme–phoneme correspondences – 'grotty graphemes'

The phonics programme Read Write Inc. uses the term 'grotty grapheme' for the graphemes which make a word 'tricky'. For example, in *said*, the *ai* in the middle is a short vowel sound rather than the long vowel sound usually made by *ai* (*rain*, *pain*, *drain* etc).

Look at the words below and identify the 'grotty graphemes':

- <u>o</u>ld: 'o' grapheme represents the long vowel sound rather than the short vowel sound.

- w<u>a</u>s: 'a' grapheme represents an 'o' sound rather than the short vowel sound it usually represents.

- ha<u>ve</u>: this is not a split digraph (see Chapter 5). Instead the 've' grapheme makes the 'v' sound.

- n<u>o</u>: 'o' grapheme represents the long vowel sound rather than the short vowel sound.

- h<u>e</u>: 'e' grapheme represents the long vowel sound rather than the short vowel sound.

- y<u>ou</u>: 'ou' grapheme represents an 'oo' sound which is a less common grapheme–phoneme correspondence and has not been taught in phase two or three.

- d<u>ay</u>: 'ay' grapheme represents an 'ai' sound. This grapheme–phoneme correspondence has not been taught in phase two or three.

- s<u>aw</u>: 'aw' grapheme represents an 'or' sound. This grapheme–phoneme correspondence has not been taught in phase two or three.

- w<u>ere</u>: 'ere' grapheme represents an 'ur' sound. This grapheme–phoneme correspondence has not been taught in phase two or three.

- y<u>our</u>: 'our' grapheme represents an 'or' sound. This grapheme–phoneme correspondence has not been taught in phase two or three.

- h<u>ere</u>: 'ere' grapheme represents an 'ear' sound. This grapheme–phoneme correspondence has not been taught in phase two or three.

- th<u>ey</u>: 'ey' grapheme represents an 'ai' sound which is a less common grapheme–phoneme correspondence and has not been taught in phase two or three.

Section 3: identifying tricky bits in the 50 most common English words

the	w<u>a</u>s	that	th<u>ere</u>	then
and	y<u>ou</u>	with	out	w<u>ere</u>
a	th<u>ey</u>	<u>a</u>ll	this	g<u>o</u>
t<u>o</u>	on	we	ha<u>ve</u>	litt<u>le</u>
s<u>ai</u>d	sh<u>e</u>	<u>are</u>	went	as
in	is	up	b<u>e</u>	n<u>o</u>
h<u>e</u>	for	had	like	mum
<u>I</u>	at	m<u>y</u>	s<u>o</u> <u>me</u>	one*
of	his	h<u>er</u>	s<u>o</u>	d<u>o</u>
it	but	<u>wh</u> <u>at</u>	not	m<u>e</u>

*It is not possible to show the phonemes represented by graphemes in the word *one*.

Section 4: exploring alternative spellings

Some possible incorrect alternatives include:

germ	jerm, jurm, jirm, gurm, girm
school	skool, skoole, skule, schule, scule, sckule, sckool, sckoole, skewl, skuel, skoul
make	maek, maik, mayk, meak, meyk
because	becos, bicos, becaus, beecos, beecoz, becoz
could	cud, culd, kud, kuld, kudd, cudd
said	sed, sedd, sayed, sead, psed, psedd (think of pseudonym)

You may have thought of others too, and you may see others when you analyse children's writing. The important thing is to check if children are hearing all the different phonemes in words when they attempt to spell them. They can go on to investigate spelling possibilities and probabilities through word sort activities and through looking at a range of texts.

What to do next?

Reinforce your knowledge and understanding of tricky words by doing as many as possible of the following:

- Observe teachers teaching children 'tricky' words and note how they help children to remember the tricky bits.

- Look at pieces of writing produced by children working in phase three of *Letters and Sounds*, or an equivalent stage in another programme, and analyse the spelling errors to consider why they may have made them and the grapheme–phoneme correspondence that they have drawn on.

- Read Chapter 3 in *Teaching Systematic Synthetic Phonics in Primary Schools* (Jolliffe *et al.*, 2012) to find out more about teaching 'tricky' words.

Websites

There are several useful websites where you can find information about tricky words:

For a further explanation of tricky words and how to teach them, see **http:// phonicbooks.wordpress.com/2012/01/16/what-is-a-tricky-word/**

Recommended reading

Jolliffe, W. (2007) *You Can Teach Synthetic Phonics*. Leamington Spa: Scholastic.

Jolliffe, W. and Waugh, D. with Carss, A. (2012) *Teaching Systematic Synthetic Phonics in Primary Schools*. London: Learning Matters/SAGE (Chapter 3).

Lewis, M. and Ellis, S. (eds) (2006) *Phonics, Practice, Research and Policy*. London: Paul Chapman.

4 Decoding and encoding text

Learning outcomes

This chapter will help you to audit your:

- understanding of the reversible processes of decoding and encoding text;
- understanding of the importance of providing opportunities for application of phonic knowledge in reading and writing;
- understanding of the role of decodable texts in the teaching of reading.

Work through each section below, responding to each question or task. When you have completed each section, you can read the answers at the end of the chapter. At the end of this chapter you can also find support for further reading and study related to decoding and encoding.

Section 1: key terminology for decoding and encoding text

It is important that you understand the terms below before you move on to the next activity. Provide a definition of each and check your definitions against those at the end of the chapter:

- decoding

- encoding

- segmenting

- blending

- synthetic phonics

- decodable texts

Section 2: application of phonic knowledge for reading/decoding

By the end of phase 3 in *Letters and Sounds*, children will have been taught the grapheme–phoneme correspondences which can be found on page 14 in Chapter 3 and the 'tricky' words below:

In Phase 2 of *Letters and Sounds* the tricky words are identified as:	*I the to go no into*
In Phase 3 of *Letters and Sounds* the tricky words are identified as:	*he she we me be was my you her they all are*

Based on these grapheme–phoneme correspondences and tricky words, try to identify words in the following text that children may find difficult to decode because they contain grapheme–phoneme correspondences or are tricky words that children have not yet been taught. Use the example below to help you:

It was a bright **sunny** **day**. **There** was not a **cloud** in the **sky**. **Both** of the children **wanted** to **play** in the paddling pool in the garden. **They** put on **their** swimming **costumes** and **jumped** into the cool **water** with a **great** splash!

Word	Decoding difficulty at this stage (underlined)	Word	Decoding difficulty at this stage (underlined)
sunn**y**	Children have only been taught the 'ee' grapheme for this phoneme.	d**ay**	Children have only been taught the 'ai' grapheme for this phoneme.
th**ere**	Children have only been taught the 'air' grapheme for this phoneme. This is a tricky word taught in phase 4.	cl**ou**d	Children have only been taught the 'ow' grapheme for this phoneme.
sk**y**	Children have only been taught the 'igh' grapheme for this phoneme.	b**o**th	Children have only been taught the 'oa' grapheme for this phoneme.
w**a**nted	It is not until phase 6 in *Letters and Sounds* that children are taught that when an /o/ phoneme follows a /w/ phoneme, it is frequently spelt with the grapheme 'a'.	pl**ay**	Children have only been taught the 'ai' grapheme for this phoneme.
th**ey**	Children have only been taught the 'ai' grapheme for this phoneme.	th**eir**	Children have only been taught the 'air' grapheme for this phoneme. This is a tricky word taught in phase 5.
cost**u**mes	Children have not yet been taught the split vowel digraph for the long vowel phoneme /ue/.	jump**ed**	Children are likely to sound out the /e/ and /d/ phoneme rather than modify it to the /t/ phoneme.
w**a**ter	It is not until phase 6 in *Letters and Sounds* that children are taught that when an /o/ phoneme follows a /w/ phoneme, it is frequently spelt with the grapheme 'a'.	gr**ea**t	Children have only been taught the 'ai' grapheme for this phoneme.

Try to do the same with the text below:

It was Bob's birthday and he was looking forward to his party. Both he and his sister were blowing up balloons to put on the gate outside, when there was a knock at the door.

Composing decodable sentences for children to read

Now try to write a few decodable sentences for a child to read. Base your word choice on their knowledge of grapheme–phoneme correspondences and tricky words by the end of phase 3 in *Letters and Sounds*. You may wish to use the example below to help you get started:

At night, the cow on the farm did not sleep. The rain ran down the barn roof until morning.

Section 3: application of phonic knowledge for spelling/encoding

Use the grapheme–phoneme correspondences which can be found on page 14 in Chapter 3 and the 'tricky' words above to rewrite the two sentences below and adapt spellings accordingly. This will entail misspelling some words, but the activity is designed to focus your attention on the kinds of spelling children may produce at this stage, when they rely upon their knowledge of one grapheme for each of the 44 phonemes.

Example
The frightened girl, who was dressed in a blue skirt, shouted at the wolf.

May be written as

The (tricky word taught in phase 2) **frightnd** (not yet been taught 'ed' suffix) **gurl, hoo was** (tricky word taught in phase 3) **dresst** (not yet been taught 'ed' suffix) **in a bloo skurt, showted** (not yet been taught 'ed' suffix but can hear the separate sounds e/d) **at the wulf.**

Note how the words *frightened*, *dressed* and *shouted* have different misspellings at the end. This is based on the sounds that children can hear for the 'ed' suffix. In phase 6 of *Letters and Sounds* children develop grammatical awareness, alongside the 'ed' suffix, in order to recognise that the word they are attempting to spell is a past tense word.

Have a go at rewriting the sentences below and consider why the child would misspell some of the words:

- The baby looked out of the window and waved at the bright yellow moon in the sky.

- At the weekend, I went to the park in the pouring rain and played on the slide with my friends.

Answers

Section 1: key terminology for decoding and encoding text

Decoding
The act of translating graphemes into phonemes – i.e. reading.

Encoding
The act of transcribing units of sound or phonemes into graphemes – i.e. spelling.

Segmenting
Splitting up a word into its individual phonemes in order to spell it – i.e. the word *pat* has three phonemes: /p/a/t/.

Blending
To draw individual sounds together to pronounce a word – e.g. /c/l/a/p/ blended together reads *clap*.

Synthetic phonics
Synthetic phonics involves separating words into phonemes and then blending the phonemes together to read the word. This compares with analytic phonics in which segments or parts of words are analysed and patterns are compared with other words.

Decodable texts
Texts which can be easily decoded using phonic strategies available to children at a particular stage in a phonics programme – e.g. *cat*, *dog*, *lamp*.

Section 2: application of phonic knowledge for reading/decoding

You were asked to try to identify words in the following text that children may find difficult to decode because they contain grapheme–phoneme correspondences or are tricky words that children have not yet been taught:

It was Bob's **birthday** and he was looking forward to his **party**. He and his **sister were blowing** up balloons to put on the **gate outside, when there** was a **knock** at the **door**.

Word	Decoding difficulty at this stage (underlined)	Word	Decoding difficulty at this stage (underlined)
bi<u>rth</u>d<u>ay</u>	Children have only been taught the 'er' grapheme and the 'ai' grapheme for the corresponding phonemes in this word.	par<u>ty</u>	Children have only been taught the 'ee' grapheme for this phoneme.
sist<u>er</u>	Children have only been taught the 'ur' grapheme for this phoneme.	<u>were</u>	This is a tricky word taught in phase 4.
bl<u>ow</u>ing	Children have only been taught the 'oa' grapheme for this phoneme.	g<u>a</u>t<u>e</u>	Children have not yet been taught the split vowel digraph for the long vowel phoneme /ai/.
<u>out</u>s<u>i</u>de	Children have only been taught the 'ow' grapheme for this phoneme. 'Out' is a tricky word taught in phase 4. Children have not yet been taught the split vowel digraph for the long vowel phoneme /igh/.	<u>w</u>hen	Children have only been taught the 'w' grapheme for this phoneme.
th<u>ere</u>	Children have only been taught the 'air' grapheme for this phoneme. This is a tricky word taught in phase 4.	<u>kn</u>ock	Children have only been taught the 'n' grapheme for this phoneme.
d<u>oor</u>	Children have only been taught the 'or' grapheme for this phoneme.		

Section 3: application of phonic knowledge for spelling/encoding

You were asked to rewrite the sentences below and consider why the child would misspell some of the words:

The baby looked out of the window and waved at the bright yellow moon in the sky.

May be written as

The baibee lukt owt ov the windoa and waivd at the bright yelloa moon in the skigh.

I really enjoyed going to the park in the pouring rain because I played on the slide with my friends.

May be written as

I reely enjoyd goaing to the park in the poring rain beecos I plaid on the slighd with my frends.

Based on knowledge of grapheme–phoneme correspondences in phases 2 and 3 of *Letters and Sounds*, you will note that there may be more than one phonically plausible way to spell the words above (see Chapter 3).

What to do next?

Reinforce your knowledge and understanding of decoding and encoding by doing as many as possible of the following:

- Analyse a decodable text against the corresponding stage within the phonics programme it is designed for, to identify why it is decodable for children at that particular stage.

- Compose a piece of decodable text for a child working within phase 4 in *Letters and Sounds*, or an equivalent stage in another programme, and see if the child is able to decode it.

- Read Chapter 4 in *Teaching Systematic Synthetic Phonics in Primary Schools* (Jolliffe *et al.*, 2012) to find out more about decoding and encoding.

Websites

There are several useful websites including for practical activities:

The Florida Center for Reading Research (**http://www.fcrr.org/Curriculum/pdf/ GK-1/P_Final_Part4.pdf**).

Recommended reading

Jolliffe, W. and Waugh, D. with Carss, A. (2012) *Teaching Systematic Synthetic Phonics in Primary Schools*. London: Learning Matters/SAGE (Chapter 4).

McGuinness, D. (2004) *Early Reading Instruction: what science really tells us about how to teach reading*. Cambridge, MA: MIT Press. Read this book to explore in more detail the importance of decoding and encoding and how these need to be constantly and reversibly applied.

5 Long vowel digraphs

Learning outcomes

This chapter will help you to audit your:

- understanding of the features of the advanced alphabetic code;
- understanding of vowel digraphs, including the most common spelling choices and alternative pronunciations;
- understanding of vowel digraphs for long and short vowel phonemes;
- understanding of the split digraph.

Work through each section below, responding to each question or task. When you have completed each section, you can read the answers at the end of the chapter. At the end of this chapter you can also find support for further reading and study related to vowel digraphs.

Section 1: key terminology for vowel digraphs

It is important that you understand the terms below before you move on to the next activity. Provide a definition of each and check your definitions against those at the end of the chapter:

- vowel digraph

- long vowel phoneme

- short vowel phoneme

- split digraph

- trigraph

- quadgraph

Section 2: vowel digraphs

A digraph is two letters that are combined to produce one phoneme – e.g. *ee, ch, ow*. Vowel digraphs can represent a short vowel phoneme – e.g. br<u>ea</u>d, l<u>oo</u>k. Can you identify the vowel digraphs representing a short vowel phoneme in the words below?

said	head	rough	instead	cough

Vowel digraphs can represent a long vowel phoneme – e.g. r<u>ai</u>n. Can you identify the vowel digraphs representing a long vowel phoneme in the words below?

meet	rain	goat	argue	blow

Split digraphs represent the long vowel phoneme, but the two letters are split by another letter (a consonant), e.g. m<u>a</u>k<u>e</u>, l<u>i</u>n<u>e</u>, h<u>o</u>m<u>e</u>. Can you identify the split digraphs in the words below?

kite	late	note	bike	discrete

Now sort the words below, taken from Year 1 in the National Curriculum (NC), into three sets of vowel digraphs representing short vowel phonemes, long vowel phonemes and split digraphs.

> sail, clue, slide, slow, road, field, new, goes, sea, lake, hole, join, day, bite, ready, dream, pie, home, true, tame, play, bone, few, time, tree, dead, soap, theme

Section 3: identifying vowel digraphs in the Years 3–4 spelling list

Look at the example words below taken from the draft NC at Years 3–4. Identify which words contain a vowel digraph. This could be a long vowel phoneme, a short vowel phoneme, or it could be a split digraph.

> accident, advertise, benefit, breath, building, chocolate, congratulate, describe, difficult, experiment, extreme, independent, nephew, often, possess, punctuate, separate, sew, surprise

Section 4: create a long vowel phoneme chart

There are a many different graphemes that represent a long vowel phoneme. It might be a one (m<u>i</u>nd), two (d<u>ay</u>), three (h<u>igh</u>) or even four (<u>eigh</u>t) letter grapheme.

Sort the words below into the correct columns based on the long vowel phoneme each contains. This may be represented by a number of different graphemes. There are some examples, already in the table, to help you:

t<u>oy</u>, she, c<u>oa</u>t, t<u>i</u>me, n<u>ow</u>, baby, d<u>ough</u>, me, b<u>ow</u>l, lake, tiger, st<u>ay</u>, b<u>oi</u>l, h<u>ea</u>t, p<u>ie</u>, b<u>ough</u>, b<u>oa</u>t, gr<u>ey</u>, st<u>ea</u>k, j<u>oy</u>, br<u>ow</u>n, str<u>aigh</u>t, f<u>igh</u>t, st<u>ea</u>l, b<u>o</u>n<u>e</u>, discr<u>e</u>t<u>e</u>, sh<u>y</u>, l<u>ou</u>d, sl<u>eigh</u>, c<u>o</u>n<u>e</u>

/ee/	/ie/	/oe/	/ae/	/ow/	/oi/
f<u>ee</u>l	t<u>ie</u>	t<u>oe</u>	play	c<u>ow</u>	c<u>oi</u>n
w<u>ea</u>k	k<u>i</u>nd	bl<u>ow</u>	rain	r<u>ou</u>nd	b<u>oy</u>

Answers

Section 1: key terminology for vowel digraphs

- **Vowel digraph:** two letters that are combined to produce a long or a short vowel phoneme.

- **Long vowel phoneme:** the long vowel sounds as in *feel* or *cold*.

- **Short vowel phoneme:** the short vowel sounds as in *hat* or *said*.

- **Split digraph:** two letters, making one sound, but separated by a consonant – e.g. *a-e* as in *cake*.

- **Trigraph:** three letters which combine to make a new sound, e.g. h**air**.

- **Quadgraph:** four letters which combine to make a new sound, e.g. th**ough**t.

Section 2: vowel digraphs

You were asked to identify the vowel digraphs representing a short vowel phoneme in the words below:

s**ai**d	h**ea**d	r**ou**gh	inst**ea**d	c**ou**gh

You were asked to identify the vowel digraphs representing a long vowel phoneme in the words below. Note that some vowel digraphs include consonants – e.g. *ar*, *ow*.

m**ee**t	r**ai**n	g**oa**t	arg**ue**	bl**ow**

You were asked to identify the split digraphs in the words below:

k**i_e**	l**a_e**	n**o_e**	b**i_e**	discr**e_e**

You were asked to sort the words below, taken from Year 1 in the NC, into vowel digraphs representing short vowel phonemes, long vowel phonemes and split digraphs:

Short vowel digraphs	r**ea**dy, d**ea**d
Long vowel digraphs	s**ai**l, cl**ue**, sl**ow**, r**oa**d, f**ie**ld, n**ew**, g**oe**s, s**ea**, j**oi**n, d**ay**, dr**ea**m, p**ie**, tr**ue**, pl**ay**, f**ew**, tr**ee**, s**oa**p
Split vowel digraphs	sl**i_e**, l**a_e**, h**o_e**, b**i_e**, h**o_e**, t**a_e**, b**o_e**, t**i_e**, th**e_e**

Section 3: identifying vowel digraphs in the Years 3–4 spelling list

You were asked to look at the example words below taken from the draft NC at Years 3–4, and to identify which words contain a vowel digraph. The vowel digraphs could represent a long vowel phoneme, a short vowel phoneme or could be a split digraph. The words with vowel digraphs appear in bold with the digraphs underlined:

accident, **advertise**, benefit, **breath**, **building**, **chocolate**, **congratulate**, **describe**, difficult, experiment, **extreme**, independent, **nephew**, often, possess, **punctuate**, **separate**, **sew**, surprise

Section 4: create a long vowel phoneme chart

You were asked to sort the words below into the correct columns based on the long vowel phoneme each contains. This may be represented by a number of different graphemes:

/ee/	/ie/	/oe/	/ae/	/ow/	/oi/
feel	tie	toe	play	cow	coin
weak	kind	blow	rain	round	boy
she	time	coat	baby	now	toy
me	tiger	dough	lake	bough	boil
heat	pie	bowl	stay	brown	joy
steal	fight	boat	grey	loud	
discrete	shy	bone	steak		
		cone	straight		
			sleigh		

What to do next?

Reinforce your knowledge and understanding of vowel digraphs by doing as many as possible of the following:

- Observe teachers teaching vowel digraphs. Note whether they represent a long or short vowel phoneme. Collect a bank of ideas and activities for teaching vowel digraphs and the split digraph.

- Read Chapter 5 in *Teaching Systematic Synthetic Phonics in Primary Schools* (Jolliffe *et al.*, 2012) to find out more about long vowel phonemes and the multiple spelling choices.

- Create your own long vowel phoneme chart (as in section 4) and add to it whenever you come across words containing a long vowel phoneme. This will form a useful point of reference for you.

Websites

There are several useful websites, including:

Interactive Reading Games: Long Vowel Phonemes **http://www.roythezebra.com/ reading-games-long-vowel-phonemes.html**.

Free worksheets, interactive activities and other resources to help children learn vowel phonemes **http://www.galacticphonics.com/longvowels/long.htm**.

Long vowel phonemes activities from NGfL Cymru **https://hwb.wales.gov.uk/cms/hwbcontent/Shared%20Documents/vtc/16022007/wordmaker_vowels1/lesson.html**.

A range of activities and resources to teach long and short vowel phonemes in Key Stage 2 **www.ks2phonics.org.uk**.

Recommended reading

DCSF (2007) *Letters and Sounds: principles and practice of high quality phonics*. London: DCSF.

DCSF (2009) *Support for Spelling*. London: DCSF.

Jolliffe, W. (2007) *You Can Teach Synthetic Phonics*. Leamington Spa: Scholastic.

Jolliffe, W. and Waugh, D. with Carss, A. (2012) *Teaching Systematic Synthetic Phonics in Primary Schools*. London: Learning Matters/SAGE (Chapter 5).

6 Spelling

Work through each section below, responding to each question or task. When you have completed each section, you can read the answers at the end of the chapter. At the end of this chapter you can also find support for further reading and study related to spelling.

Section 1: key terminology for spelling

It is important that you understand the terms below before you move on to the next activity. Provide a definition of each and check your definitions against those at the end of the chapter:

- singular
- plural
- morpheme
- prefix
- suffix
- homonyms
- homophones
- homographs
- compound word
- medial vowel sound

Section 2: sorting words according to medial vowel sound

Sort the words below into groups according to their medial vowel sound:

mat   bed   pig   dog   sun   bag   pen   sit   box   cup
        bull   frog   fan   bed   mint

Section 3: modifying words (see also Chapter 12)

Look at the words from the draft NC listed below which are to be learnt in Years
3–4. How many could **not** be added to or modified to create new words? Remember,
you can often make the words into plurals (e.g. accidents), change nouns to verbs
(e.g. bicycle into bicycling), change verbs to nouns (e.g. approve to approval), change
adjectives to nouns (e.g. difficult to difficulty) etc.

---

accident, advertise, approve, benefit, behave, bicycle, breath, breathe, building, calendar, certain,
concentrate, chocolate, congratulate, conscience, continue, decorate, describe, dictionary, difficult,
discover, disturb, early, earn, earth, educate, excite, experience, experiment, explore, extreme, February,
grammar, guide, guard, half, heart, immediate, improve, increase, independent, injure, inquire, interest,
island, junior, knowledge, library, material, medicine, mention, multiply, murmur, nephew, occasion,
often, opposite, paragraph, particular, peculiar, position, possess, produce, professor, promise, property,
prove, punctuate, quality, quantity, quarrel, quarter, recite, recover, register, regular, reign, remember,
sentence, separate, sew, situate, strength, sufficient, sure, surprise, surround, thought, though, weary

Now see how many words you can create from the 90 above.

What does this activity tell you about teaching vocabulary and spelling?

Section 4: compound words

Compound words are made up of at least two other words – for example, foot and
ball make football, and head and teacher make headteacher. Look at the compound
words below and separate them into their constituent parts. The first one has been
done for you:

- *everyone*   *every + one*

- *everybody*

- *somewhere*

- *anyone*

- *everything*

- *nowhere*

- *nobody*

- *anywhere*

- *anybody*

- *someone*

Now look at the table below and see how many compound words you can create using each word as many times as you like:

head	ball	house	hand
ache	tooth	foot	teacher
green	brush	hair	day
birth	play	week	farm

Section 5: homonyms, homophones and homographs

Look at the words below and decide which are homonyms, which are homophones, and which are homographs:

see   sea   record   fast   hoarse   cricket   weather   lead   flee   flew

Section 6: spelling rules and generalisations

Look at the words below, all of which are spelled correctly, and work out a spelling rule for making words which end with *y* into plurals:

monkeys   babies   keys   ladies   days   hobbies   buggies

Look at the words below, all of which are spelled correctly, and work out a spelling rule for adding *-ing* to words:

liking   running   dying   seeing   swimming   hoping   hopping   saving   loving

Now work out rules and generalisations which you could teach to children to complete the following:

- English words don't end with _____. (give as many letters as possible)

- Q is almost always _____.

- There are many ways to make the /c/ sound in *cat* (e.g. *k*, *ck*), but the following are never found at the beginnings of words: _____.

- Think about the spelling 'rule' which most people know: 'i before e except after c.' Is this a good rule? Are there exceptions? How could you modify the rule to make it clearer?

Answers

Section 1: key terminology for spelling

Singular

A word form used to refer to one of something. When more than one is referred to, a plural form is used. Nouns can be singular or plural.

Plural

The plural forms of words show that they refer to more than one item. This usually involves adding an *s* (*cats*, *books*) or *es* (*matches*, *buses*), but some plurals are irregular. For example, *child* becomes *children*, *mouse* becomes *mice* and *goose* becomes *geese*.

Some nouns remain the same in their plural form as in their singular form, including sheep and the names of many fish (one haddock, two haddock, one salmon, two salmon).

Morpheme

The smallest unit of language that can convey meaning. A morpheme cannot be broken down into anything smaller that has a meaning. A word may consist of one morpheme ('need'), two morphemes ('need/less', 'need/ing') or three or more morphemes ('un/happi/ness'). Suffixes and prefixes are morphemes.

Prefix

Morphemes which are placed at the beginning of a word to modify or change its meaning. For example, dis/like, micro/scope, tri/cycle.

Suffix

Morphemes added to the ends of words to modify their meanings. For example, use and useful or useless; look and looking, looks or looked.

Homonyms

Words with the same spelling and pronunciation but different meanings, for example, left (opposite of right) and left (departed), bark (of a dog) and bark (of a tree). The term 'homonym' is often used as a general term for homophones and homographs. Homonym means 'same name'.

Homophones

Words which sound the same but have different spellings and meanings are homophones (homo – same, phone – sound). For example sea and see, sew, so and sow, blue and blew, great and grate. Homophone means 'same sound'.

Homographs

Words which are spelled the same as other words which mean something different and are pronounced differently. For example, sow (spreading seeds) and sow (a female pig); lead (to take charge or something used to restrain a dog) and lead (a heavy metal), row (argue) and row (in a boat). Homograph means 'same writing'.

Compound word

A word made when two words are joined to form a new word – for example, toothbrush, football, toenail. Hyphens are sometimes used to link the two parts of the word – for example, twenty-seven, self-audit, penalty-taker.

Medial vowel sound

The medial vowel sound is the sound of the phoneme in the middle of a word, so that hot and cot have the same medial vowel sound.

Section 2: sorting words according to medial vowel sound

You were asked to sort the words below into groups according to their medial vowel sound. For the words you were given, the groups should be as follows:

mat	*bet*	*pig*	*dog*	*sun*
bag	*pen*	*sit*	*box*	*cup*
fan	*bed*	*mint*	*frog*	*bull*

As children's phonic skills develop they will encounter words in which the medial vowel sounds are the same, but they are spelled differently. For example:

- *bed* and *head*

- *hit* and *hymn*

- *dog* and *was*

By developing children's awareness of medial sounds, as well as initial and final sounds, we help them to develop their phonological awareness and their phonemic awareness (see Chapter 1).

Section 3: modifying words (see also Chapter 12)

Look at the first ten words in the list:

accident, advertise, approve, benefit, behave, bicycle, breath, breathe, building, calendar

All can be modified by adding prefixes and/or suffixes (morphemes). Some examples are given below:

- *accidents, accidental, accidentally*

- *advertises, advertising, advertised, advertisement*

- *approves, approved, approval, approving, disapprove*

- *benefits, benefited, benefiting*

- *behaves, behaved, behaviour, behaving*

- *bicycles, bicycles, bicycled, bicycling*

- *breaths, breathing, breathed*

- *breathes, breathing*

- *buildings, rebuild, rebuilding*

- *calendars*

All the words in the list of 90 can be modified in some way – often in several ways. When we tried this out with our trainees, the words they found most difficulty in modifying were *February* and *often*, but more than one *February* would be *Februaries* (I remember three *Februaries* ago... or I have lived through some very cold *Februaries*), and *often* can become *oftener*, even though we more often use *more often*!

What all this tells us is that when we teach spellings we should not only focus on individual words, but should also look at how they can be modified to make new words. This will teach children about spelling conventions such as adding *-ing* and *-ed*, and making plurals, and will also broaden their vocabularies and their understanding of how words work. Even if children learned ten new words every week from Year 1 to Year 6 they would only learn around 2500, which is far fewer than they will actually need. Therefore, we need to help them develop an understanding of words and spelling which will enable them to apply their knowledge and understanding to unfamiliar words.

Section 4: compound words

The compound words can be divided as follows:

- *everyone*   *every + one*
- *everybody*   *every + body*
- *somewhere*   *some + where*
- *anyone*   *any + one*
- *everything*   *every + thing*
- *nowhere*   *no + where*
- *nobody*   *no + body*
- *anywhere*   *any + where*
- *anybody*   *any + body*
- *someone*   *some + one*

You were asked to look at the table below and see how many compound words you could create using each word as many times as you liked:

head	ball	house	hand
ache	tooth	foot	teacher
green	brush	hair	day
birth	play	week	farm

Possibilities include:

headache, headteacher, handball, greenhouse, football, toothache, toothbrush, hairbrush, birthday, weekday, farmhouse, farmhand

Children encounter lots of compound words in their reading. By helping them to see how these words are created, we can help them to break them down to read and understand them. New compound words are often created for new inventions or situations and many are then included in dictionaries (for example, jobseeker, supersaver, masterchef).

Section 5: homonyms, homophones and homographs

You were asked to look at the words below and decide which are homonyms, which are homophones, and which are homographs:

see   sea   record   fast   hoarse   cricket   weather   lead   flee   flew

See and *sea* are homophones because they sound the same but are spelled differently.

- *Hoarse* is a homophone for *horse*.
- *Weather* is a homophone for *whether*.
- *Flee* is a homophone for *flea*.
- *Flew* is a homophone for *flu*.
- *Record* is a homograph because it can be pronounced in more than one way – for example, I record my favourite programme. Mo broke the record.
- *Lead* is a homograph because it can be pronounced in more than one way – for example, My dog has a lead. The lead was stolen from the roof.
- *Cricket* is a homonym (it can be a sport or an insect).
- *Fast* is a homonym (it can mean to go without food or quick).

Section 6: spelling rules and generalisations

- If a word ends with a vowel before the *y*, add an *s* (*keys, days*).
- If a word has a consonant before the *y*, replace the *y* with *ies* (*baby – babies, hobby – hobbies*).

Spelling rules for adding *-ing* to words:

- For words which end with *y* just add *-ing* (*worrying, marrying*).
- If the word ends in *e*, drop the *e* and add *-ing* (*have – having, bite – biting*).

- If the word is short and ends with a vowel and then a consonant, double the consonant and add *-ing* (*run – running, hop – hopping*).

Others:

- If a word has a double *e*, do not drop the second *e* (*free + ing – freeing*).

- Change *ie* to *y* before adding *-ing* (*die + ing = dying, lie + ing = lying*).

Rules and generalisations which you could teach to children include the following:

- English words don't end with *j, v, q* (you were asked to give as many letters as possible).

- *Q* is almost always followed by *u* (exceptions such as Iraq and Qatar are not English words).

- There are many ways to make the /c/ sound in *cat* (e.g. *k, ck, cc, q* (in Iraq), *que* in cheque and plaque, *ch* in chemistry), but the following are never found at the beginnings of words: *ck, cc*.

- Think about the spelling 'rule' which most people know: 'i before e except after c.' Is this a good rule? No, because there are so many common exceptions – their, seeing, being, rein, reign, weigh, height, heir, reinforce etc. Are there exceptions (see above)? How could you modify the rule to make it clearer? If you modify the rule to 'i before e except after c when the word rhymes with me' there are fewer exceptions.

What to do next?

Develop your knowledge and understanding of spelling by:

- Exploring morphemes and their meanings.

- Making collections of homographs, homophones and homonyms – you can find these on websites.

- Finding examples of compound words and creating games and activities.

- Making collections of unusual grapheme–phoneme correspondences, for example in names.

- Considering the value of different spelling rules and generalisations.

Websites

There are several useful websites, including:

UCL's Spelling Introduction (**http://www.phon.ucl.ac.uk/home/dick/tta/spelling/spelling.htm**).

Recommended reading

DCSF (2009) *Support for Spelling*. Norwich: DfES.

Gentry, R. (1987) *Spel… is a Four-letter Word*. London: Heinemann.

Jolliffe, W. and Waugh, D. with Carss, A. (2012) *Teaching Systematic Synthetic Phonics in Primary Schools*. London: Learning Matters/SAGE (Chapter 6).

Mudd, N. (1994) *Effective Spelling: a practical guide for teachers*. London: Hodder & Stoughton.

Reason, R. and Boote, R. (1994) *Helping Children with Reading and Spelling*. London: Routledge. This is an excellent book which is well worth seeking out.

Waugh, D. and Jolliffe, W. (2012) *English 5–11*. London: Routledge (Chapter 12).

Waugh, D., Warner, C. and Waugh, R. (2013) *Spelling, Grammar and Punctuation*. London: Learning Matters/SAGE (Chapters 2, 3, 4 and 5).

Wray, D. and Medwell, J. (2008) *Primary English: Extending Knowledge in Practice*. London: Learning Matters/SAGE. See Chapter 4 for an interesting look at strategies for learning spellings and investigating spellings with your class.

7 Teaching phonics in the early years

> **Learning outcomes**
>
> This chapter will help you to audit your:
>
> - understanding of methods of teaching phonics linked to a broad and rich language curriculum;
> - knowledge of appropriate and engaging methods for teaching phonics in the early years;
> - understanding of key features of effective practice when teaching phonics in the early years.

Work through each section below, responding to each question or task. When you have completed each section, you can read the answers at the end of the chapter. At the end of this chapter you can also find support for further reading and study related to phonics in the early years.

Section 1: key terminology for phonics in the early years

It is important that you understand the terms below before you move on to the next activity. Provide a definition of each and check your definitions against those at the end of the chapter:

- language-rich curriculum

- quality first teaching

- phonological awareness

- oral segmenting and blending

- general sound discrimination

- alliteration

- voice sounds

Section 2: The Independent Review of the Teaching of Early Reading (The Rose Review)

Access the review through the web link below and read Aspect 2 (pp. 29–35):

http://webarchive.nationalarchives.gov.uk/20130401151715/https://www.education.gov.uk/publications/eOrderingDownload/0201-2006PDF-EN-01.pdf

Now complete the activity below. Why does Rose think these are so significant in the teaching of early reading?

- speaking and listening

- language-rich curriculum

- quality first teaching

- discrete teaching of phonics

Section 3: phonological awareness

Phonological awareness is an important prerequisite for successful reading development. In most systematic synthetic phonics programmes, the early phases focus on developing children's phonological awareness. Phase 1 in *Letters and Sounds* includes a range of activities, designed to develop phonological awareness, that are separated into seven aspects:

- Aspect 1: general sound discrimination – environmental sounds.

- Aspect 2: general sound discrimination – instrumental sounds.

- Aspect 3: general sound discrimination – body percussion.

- Aspect 4: rhythm and rhyme.

- Aspect 5: alliteration.

- Aspect 6: voice sounds.

- Aspect 7: oral blending and segmenting.

Read the description of the activities below, taken from phase 1 in *Letters and Sounds*, and decide which of the aspects of phonological awareness above they are designed to teach.

Story sounds
As you read or tell stories, encourage the children to play their instruments in different ways (e.g. *Make this instrument sound like giant's footsteps,... a fairy fluttering,... a cat pouncing,... an elephant stamping*). Invite them to make their own suggestions for different characters (e.g. *How might Jack's feet sound as he tiptoes by the sleeping giant? And what about when he runs fast to escape down the beanstalk?*). As the children become familiar with the pattern of the story, each child could be responsible for a different sound.

I spy
Place on the floor or on a table a selection of objects with names containing two or three phonemes (e.g. zip, hat, comb, cup, chain, boat, tap, ball). Check that all the children know the names of the objects. Then you or perhaps a puppet say *I spy with*

my little eye a z-i-p. Then invite a child to say the name of the object and hold it up. All the children can then say the individual phonemes and blend them together: 'z-i-p, zip.' When the children have become familiar with this game, use objects with names that start with the same initial phoneme (e.g. cat, cap, cup, cot, comb, kite). This will really encourage the children to listen and then blend right through the word, rather than relying on the initial sound.

Playing with words

Gather together a set of familiar objects with names that have varying syllable patterns (e.g. pencil, umbrella, camera, xylophone). Show the objects to the children, name them, and talk about what they are used for. Wait for the children to share some of their experiences of the objects; for instance, some of them will have used a camera. Then encourage them to think about how the name of the object sounds and feels as they say it. Think about the syllables and clap them out as you say each word. Then clap the syllables for a word without saying it and ask: *What object could that be?*

As children gain confidence, try some long words like *binoculars, telephone, dinosaur*.

Bertha goes to the zoo

Set up a small toy zoo and join the children as they play with it. Use a toy bus and a bag of animal toys with names starting with the same sound (e.g. a lion, a lizard, a leopard, a llama and a lobster) to act out this story. Chant the following rhyme and allow each child in turn to draw an animal out of the bag and add an animal name to the list of animals spotted at the zoo:

Bertha the bus is going to the zoo, Who does she see as she passes through?... a pig, a panda, a parrot and a polar bear.

Section 4: the power of play

Design a different activity for each of the areas below to teach the skill of oral blending:

- sand/water area

- role-play area

- small world area e.g. vehicles, animals etc...

- listening area

Answers

Section 1: key terminology for phonics in the early years

Language-rich curriculum

A curriculum that has speaking and listening at its centre. Links are made between language and practical experiences. It provides an environment rich in print and provides many opportunities to engage with books.

Quality first teaching
Quality first teaching includes a blend of whole-class, group and individual activities designed to match work to children's different but developing abilities.

Phonological awareness
The ability to attend to the phonological or sound structure of language as distinct from its meaning.

Oral segmenting and blending
Blending and segmenting words without using knowledge of grapheme–phoneme correspondence – i.e. without showing written forms.

General sound discrimination
The process of allowing children to become attuned to the sounds around them.

Alliteration
A sequence of words beginning with the same sound – for example, 'seven silly sailors sat upon a seat'.

Voice sounds
In early stages of phonological development children engage in activities to help them distinguish between different vocal sounds. This might include oral blending and segmenting.

Section 2: The Independent Review of the Teaching of Early Reading (The Rose Review)

You were asked why Rose maintains the following are so significant in the teaching of early reading:

Speaking and listening
Phonics involves both auditory and oral skills. Developing speaking and listening skills develops children's vocabulary and helps them to learn to listen attentively and speak confidently. Children will find decoding words that are already part of their vocabulary easier than those that are not. Their listening skills will be needed to enable them to hear the separate phonemes in words.

Language-rich curriculum
A language-rich curriculum includes the use of play, story, songs, rhymes and drama. These familiarise children with letters, words and sounds. Both their vocabulary and interest in reading are developed through allowing them time to talk with adults and each other about feelings and experiences.

Quality first teaching
Quality first teaching matches work to children's different but developing abilities. It supports the identification of children who demonstrate potential difficulties

with reading. It involves providing appropriate support which minimises the risk of children falling behind. Quality first teaching includes a blend of whole-class, group and individual work.

Discrete teaching of phonics

Teaching phonics discretely allows children to focus on word recognition skills, for reading and spelling, without being distracted by other aspects such as reading for meaning. This is a time-limited approach which will eventually be taken over by work which develops comprehension.

Section 3: phonological awareness

You were asked to read the description of the activities, take from phase 1 in *Letters and Sounds*, and decide which of the aspects of phonological awareness they are designed to teach.

Activity	Aspect of phonological awareness
Story sounds	Aspect 2: general sound discrimination – instrumental sounds
I spy	Aspect 7: oral blending and segmenting
Playing with words	Aspect 4: rhythm and rhyme
Bertha goes to the zoo	Aspect 5: alliteration

Section 4: the power of play

You were asked to design a different activity for each of the areas below to teach the skill of oral blending. Suggested activities are shown below, but you may have thought of others which are just as good:

Area	Activity to teach the skill of oral blending
Sand/water area	Hide some farm animals in the sand tray (e.g. sheep, pig, goat). Ask the children to see if they can find the sh-ee-p. The children need to blend the phonemes to work out which animal they are to look for. They then look for the corresponding animal in the sand tray. Continue by sounding out the names of the other animals.
Role-play area	Set up the role-play area as a café. Pretend to be a customer but when you order say 'I would like a cup of t-ea please' and ask the child to tell you what you have ordered. Continue ordering things but sounds them out and allow the child to blend in order to work out what you have ordered.
Small world area	Use the farm animals and a tractor and trailer. Ask the child (in role as the farmer) to collect the p-i-g and put it in the field. The child has to blend the phonemes to work out which animal needs to go into the field, collects it with the tractor and trailer and places it in the field.
Listening area	Record a popular story and laminate some pictures from it. When you record the story, sound some words out (e.g. Tom went to the p-ar-k). Leave time for the child to find the corresponding picture as part of your recording. At the end of the story the child should have the correct pictures for the words that you sounded out in.

What to do next?

Reinforce your knowledge and understanding of teaching phonics in the early years by doing as many as possible of the following:

- Spend some time in an early years setting. Note any activities in which children's phonological awareness is being developed. You can use the seven aspects in phase 1 of *Letters and Sounds* to help you.

- Read Chapter 7 in *Teaching Systematic Synthetic Phonics in Primary Schools* (Jolliffe *et al.*, 2012) to find out more about teaching phonics in the early years within a broad and rich language curriculum.

- Observe adult/child interaction and consider how it is developing speaking and listening skills and vocabulary development.

Websites

There are several useful websites:

Phonological awareness activities for the Foundation Stage (**http://www.plymouth. gov.uk/foundation_auditory_discrimination.pdf**).

Letters and Sounds phase 1 (**http://www.letters-and-sounds.com/phase-1.html**).

Recommended reading

DCSF (2007) *Letters and Sounds: principles and practice of high quality phonics*. London: DCSF.

Jolliffe, W. and Waugh, D. with Carss, A. (2012) *Teaching Systematic Synthetic Phonics in Primary Schools*. London: Learning Matters/SAGE (Chapter 7).

Literacy in Early Childhood and Primary Education (3–8 years) (2012) (Research conducted on behalf of the National Council for Curriculum and Assessment). Available at **http://www.ncca.ie/en/Curriculum_and_Assessment/Early_ Childhood_and_Primary_Education/Primary_School_Curriculum/ Language_Curriculum_Research_Reports_/litreport.pdf**.

Northern Ireland Curriculum: Language and Literacy in the Foundation Stage: phonological awareness (n.d.). Available at **http://www.nicurriculum.org.uk/docs/ foundation_stage/areas_of_learning/language_and_literacy/LL_PhonoAware. pdf**.

Whitehead, M. (2010) *Language and Literacy in the Early Years* (4th edn). London: SAGE. See this book for detailed guidance on providing a language-rich curriculum.

8 Multisensory approaches

	Learning outcomes

Learning outcomes

This chapter will help you to audit your:

- knowledge of a range of interactive and multisensory methods that will enhance (but not dominate) the teaching of phonics;
- knowledge of a range of resources, including puppets, interactive whiteboards, magnetic and electronic resources to support multisensory and interactive approaches to teaching and learning phonics.

Work through each section below, responding to each question or task. When you have completed each section, you can read the answers at the end of the chapter. At the end of this chapter you can also find support for further reading and study related to multisensory approaches.

Section 1: key terminology for multisensory approaches

What is meant by a multisensory approach to teaching phonics and reading? It is important that you understand the terms below before you move on to the next activity. Provide a definition of each and check your definitions against those at the end of the chapter:

- visual

- auditory

- kinaesthetic

- multisensory classroom environment

- interactive approaches to phonics

Section 2: phonics scenarios

Consider each of the following scenarios and decide how you could use multisensory approaches to enhance teaching and learning:

- A lesson to develop blending of phonemes for the following letters: *s a t p i n*.

- A lesson to develop understanding of consonant digraphs *ch sh th*.

- A lesson to develop understanding of the split vowel digraph.

Section 3: case study of teaching

Read the case study of a phonics lesson and identify where the teacher uses visual, auditory and kinaesthetic approaches:

> *Tina wanted to reinforce her Y1 class's ability to segment and blend so she created the Phonics Fairy who wore a cloak and held a magic wand. For phonics lessons, Tina donned the cloak and explained that the children were going to play pass the parcel but instead of passing a parcel they were going to pass a box of words. When the music stopped the person holding the box had to take a word out and segment it (i.e. l-o-g rather than reading the word log). The Phonics Fairy then waved the magic blending wand and said the word. After a while some of the more able children took turns to wear the cloak and become the Phonics Fairy.*
>
> *In subsequent lessons, Tina placed verbs in the box and explained that when the music stopped the person holding the box had to look at a word but not show it to anyone, and then mime an action. She included verbs such as hop, wave, stamp and clap. After the mime children had to raise their hands and ask what the word was by segmenting their suggestions – for example, 'Is it s-t-a-m-p?' The Phonics Fairy would then blend the phonemes to make the word and ask the child who had mimed if that was correct.*

Answers

Section 1: key terminology for multisensory approaches

What is meant by a multisensory approach to teaching phonics and reading? You were asked to define the following key terms:

Visual
Visual approaches to phonics involve activities which encourage children to look at different resources, graphemes etc.

Auditory
Visual approaches to phonics involve activities which encourage children to listen to different resources, phonemes etc.

Kinaesthetic
Some people learn better using some form of physical (kinaesthetic) activity: hence the use of actions to accompany phonemes and graphemes in Jolly Phonics.

Multisensory classroom environment
A classroom in which children can use all of a range of senses (hearing, seeing, feeling, moving).

Interactive approaches to phonics

An interactive approach ensures that children are actively involved in their learning and take a full part in lessons.

Section 2: phonics scenarios

You were asked to consider each of the following scenarios and decide how you could use multisensory approaches to enhance teaching and learning. We hope you will find the suggestions below helpful, but do try to develop and modify them to meet your class's needs.

A lesson to develop blending of phonemes for s a t p i n

Try making large cards with a letter on each. Ask six children to come to the front of the class and to stand in a line. Ask the rest of the class to suggest ways in which groups of three children holding cards could arrange themselves to make words (for example, sat, pin, nip, tap, tan). Ask another child to write the words on the board and have a class competition to see how many can be made. Each time a word is made, ask the children to segment it and then blend it into a whole word.

A lesson to develop understanding of consonant digraphs ch sh th

Try collecting pictures and small objects which include the diagraphs, *th*, *sh* and *ch*. Give each child three cards with one of the digraphs on each card. Put the pictures and objects in a large box and then take them out one at a time and ask questions such as: Which grapheme does this begin with? Which grapheme does this end with? Children should then hold up the correct card.

This can be developed into a more physical activity if you have a large space such as the school hall to work in. Put the graphemes on large pieces of paper on the wall in three different parts of the room. Get the children to sit around you in the middle of the room and take items out one by one and ask children to go to the part of the room where the appropriate digraph can be found. If some go to the wrong place, segment the word carefully and ask them to repeat it. Once everyone is in the right place, ask the class to segment and blend the word.

A lesson to develop understanding of the split vowel digraph

Make some cards with split digraphs ensuring the space between the vowels is sufficient to place a letter card in it. Give every child two consonant cards and ask them to practise sounding the letters.

Put the split digraph cards on the wall and ask if anyone can use both of their letters to make a word. For example, for the split digraph *a-e* someone with *s* and *m* would be able to make *same*, and for *i-e* someone with *b* and *t* could make *bite*. Each time someone can make a word, ask the children to segment and then blend it. Have a child write the words created on the board and challenge the children to see how many words they can make.

You could modify the activity by placing consonant cards in the middle of each table and asking groups to discuss which letters could be used. This could become an inter-group competition if you feel this is appropriate.

Section 3: case study of teaching

You were asked to read a case study of a phonics lesson and identify where the teacher uses visual, auditory and kinaesthetic approaches:

- Auditory approaches featured throughout, especially when children listened to words being segmented and blended.

- Visual elements included reading the words from the box.

- Kinaesthetic approaches included miming the words and actions, and passing the parcel.

What to do next?

Reinforce your knowledge and understanding of decoding by doing as many as possible of the following:

- Observe phonics lessons in school and make a note of the multisensory strategies used by teachers.

- Look at worksheets for phonics lessons and see how you could teach the same things using interactive and multisensory methods.

- Build up a bank of resources to support multisensory teaching and learning. These do not need to be very sophisticated and might include: grapheme cards with single letters and digraphs; split digraph cards; a collection of pictures and objects; sand trays for finger writing letters.

Websites

There are several useful websites, including:

A Whole School Approach to Phonics (**http://wsassets.s3.amazonaws.com/ws/tlr/ files/downloads/pdf/42522_book.pdf**).

Helping Every Child to Read (**http://www.helpingeverychildtoread.com/index. php/causes-of-difficulty/reading-theories/kinesthetic-approaches**).

Recommended reading

DCSF (2007) *Letters and Sounds: principles and practice of high quality phonics*. London: DCSF.

Glazzard, J. and Stokoe, J. (2013) *Teaching Systematic Synthetic Phonics and Early English*. Northwich: Critical Publishing (Chapter 5).

Jolliffe, W. and Waugh, D. with Carss, A. (2012) *Teaching Systematic Synthetic Phonics in Primary Schools*. London: Learning Matters/SAGE (Chapter 8).

9 Teaching a systematic and structured programme

Learning outcomes	

This chapter will help you to audit your:

- understanding of the essential components of a systematic structured phonics programme;
- knowledge of systematic and structured progression.

Work through each section below, responding to each question or task. When you have completed each section, you can read the answers at the end of the chapter. At the end of this chapter you can also find support for further reading and study related to teaching a systematic and structured programme.

Section 1: key terminology for a systematic and structured programme

It is important that you understand the terms below before you move on to the next activity. Provide a definition of each and check your definitions against those at the end of the chapter:

- fidelity to a programme
- systematic progression
- criteria for assuring high-quality phonic work

Section 2: criteria for assuring high-quality phonic work

Which of the following are included in the DfE core criteria for assuring high-quality phonic work that identifies the key features of an effective, systematic, synthetic phonics programme? Try to consider a rationale for your choices.

The programme should:

- include a variety of ready-made resources;
- teach children to blend phonemes, in order, all through a word to read it;

- teach children to remember all words by sight;

- introduced one grapheme–phoneme correspondence a week;

- teach actions for each grapheme–phoneme correspondence, to help children to remember them;

- teach all 40+ grapheme–phoneme correspondences in a clear, incremental sequence;

- teach children a range of different strategies for working out an unknown word e.g. looking at the picture, using the context of what has been read so far, thinking about what would make sense in the complete sentence;

- be designed to deliver discrete daily phonics session;

- allow children to apply their knowledge of grapheme–phoneme correspondences by reading texts which are entirely decodable;

- be designed to ensure that the vast majority of children have secured word recognition skills by the end of Key Stage 1.

Section 3: pace and progression

The second column in the grid below does not correctly correspond to the phases from *Letters and Sounds* in the first column. Try to match the statements in the second column with the correct phase, based on the expected length of time spent teaching it and to which year group.

Phase from *Letters and Sounds*	Expected length of time to be spent teaching this phase and to which year group
Phase 1	Up to 6 weeks – Reception
Phase 2	4–6 weeks – Year 1
Phase 3	Throughout Year 2
Phase 4	From Nursery and throughout all phases
Phase 5	Up to 12 weeks – end of Reception
Phase 6	Throughout Year 1

Section 4: a systematic structured approach

The table below provides an overview of the knowledge and skills taught in each of the phases in *Letters and Sounds*. As phase 1 is addressed in Chapter 7, this activity focuses on phases 2 to 6. It is important to note that phase 1 teaching should continue throughout all the phases.

Phase from *Letters and Sounds*	Knowledge of grapheme–phoneme correspondences (GPCs)	Skills of blending and segmenting with letters	High-frequency words containing GPCs not yet taught
Two	19 letters of the alphabet and one sound for each.	Move children on from oral blending and segmentation to blending and segmenting with letters. By the end of the phase many children should be able to read some vowel–consonant (VC) and consonant–vowel–consonant (CVC) words and to spell them either using magnetic letters or by writing the letters on paper or on whiteboards. During the phase they will be introduced to reading two-syllable words and simple captions.	*the, to, no, go, I*
Three	7 more letters of the alphabet. Graphemes to cover most of the phonemes not covered by single letters.	Blend and segment sounds represented by single letters and graphemes of more than one letter, including longer words (e.g. *chip, moon, night, thunder* – choice of word will depend on which GPCs have been taught). Blend to read simple captions, sentences and questions.	*he, she, we, me, be, was, my, you, her, they, all, are.* Emphasise parts of words containing known correspondences.
Four	No new GPCs.	Consolidate children's knowledge of graphemes in reading and spelling words containing adjacent consonants and polysyllabic words.	*said, so, have, little, some, come, were, there, little, one, do, when, out, what.* Again, emphasise parts of words containing known correspondences.
Five	More graphemes for the 40+ phonemes taught in phases 2 and 3; more ways of pronouncing graphemes introduced in phases 2 and 3.	Broaden knowledge of graphemes and phonemes for use in reading and spelling. Learn new graphemes and alternative pronunciations. Become quicker at recognising graphemes of more than one letter in words and at blending the phonemes they represent. When spelling words, learn to choose the appropriate graphemes to represent phonemes and begin to build word-specific knowledge of the spellings of words.	*oh, their, people, Mr, Mrs, looked, called, asked, water, where, who, again, though, through, work, mouse, many, laughed, because, different, any, eyes, friends, once, please.*
Six	Word-specific spellings – i.e. when phonemes can be spelt in more than one way, children will learn which words take which spellings (e.g. *see/sea, bed/head/said, cloud/clown*).	Increasingly fluent sounding and blending of words encountered in reading for the first time. Spelling of words with prefixes and suffixes, doubling and dropping letters where necessary (e.g. *hop/hopping, hope/hoping, hope/hopeful, carry/carried, happy/happiness*). Increasingly accurate spelling of words containing unusual GPCs (e.g. *laugh, once, two, answer, could, there*).	As needed.

Source: reproduced, with minor layout changes, from *Letters and Sounds: principles and practice of high quality phonics – notes of guidance for practitioners and teachers* (00282-2007BKT-EN). DfES (2007).

Use the table above to decide which phase the activities, taken from *Letters and Sounds*, below belong to. Try to consider a rationale, based on the knowledge and skills each is designed to teach.

Activity 1: what's in the box?

Resources

- Set of word cards giving words with adjacent consonants.

- Set of objects or pictures corresponding to the word cards, hidden in a box.

- Soft toy (optional).

Procedure

1. Display a word card.

2. Go through the letter recognition and blending process.

3. Ask the toy or a child to find the object in the box.

Activity 2: what's missing?

Resources

- Set of any six CVC objects from the role-play area (e.g. hospital: soap, pen, chart, book, mug).

- List of nine words for the teacher to read out, which includes the six objects and three additional items (e.g. bed, sheet, pill).

- Soft toy (optional).

Procedure

1. Pretext: you (or the soft toy) need to check that you have collected together all the items you need, which are written on your list.

2. Display the six objects.

3. Say one of the words on the list using sound-talk, ask the children to repeat it and then tell their partners what it is.

4. The children look at the items in front of them to see if the object is there.

Activity 3: phoneme frame

Prerequisite

The children must have an understanding of the grammar of the past tense and experience of segmenting words into phonemes.

Resources

- Set of five-box and six-box phoneme frames drawn on the whiteboard.

- Set of five-box and six-box phoneme frames, on laminated card so they can be reused, one per pair of children.

- Word cards placed in a bag (e.g. rounded, helped, turned, begged, hissed, wanted, sorted, hummed, waded, washed, hated, greased, lived, robbed, rocked, laughed, called, roasted).

Procedure

1. Pick a word card from the bag and read it out without showing the children.

2. Working with a partner, the children say the word to themselves then segment and count the phonemes. They decide which phoneme frame to use and try writing it with one phoneme in each box.

3. Say 'Show me' as the signal for the children to hold up their frames.

4. Demonstrate how to spell the word correctly using a frame on the whiteboard and ask the pairs of children to check their own spellings.

5. Repeat for about six words and look at the words that have been written.

6. What spelling pattern do they all have? Emphasise that even when the final phoneme sounds different (e.g. jumped), the spelling pattern is still the same.

7. Challenge the children to explain why this is (past tense of verbs).

8. Look closely at the phoneme frames.

9. Sometimes the *-ed* ending is two phonemes (e.g. wanted) and sometimes only one (e.g. grasped).

Activity 4: quick copy

Resources

- Words using some newly learned graphemes in which all graphemes of two or more letters are underlined (e.g. pound, light, boy, sigh, out, joy).

- Same words without the underlining (e.g. pound, light, boy, sigh, out, joy).

- Magnetic whiteboards with all the appropriate graphemes to make the words, one per child.

- Extra letters to act as foils (e.g. if the grapheme *oy* is needed, provide separate letters *o* and *y* as well).

- If custom-made graphemes are unavailable, attach letters together with sticky tape to make graphemes.

Procedure

1. Display a word in which the grapheme is underlined.

2. Ask the children to make the word as quickly as possible using their magnetic letters and saying the phonemes (e.g. *t-oy*) and then reading the word.

3. Check that, where appropriate, children are using joined letters, not the separate letters.

4. Repeat with each word with an underlined grapheme.

5. Repeat 1–4 with words without the underlined graphemes, being particularly vigilant that children identify the two-letter or three-letter graphemes in the words.

Activity 5: buried treasure

Resources

*   About eight cards, shaped and coloured like gold coins with words and nonsense words on them made up from graphemes the children have been learning (e.g. jarm, win, jowd, yes, wug, zip), buried in the sand tray.

*   Containers representing a treasure chest and a waste bin, or pictures of a treasure chest and a waste bin on large sheets of paper, placed flat on the table.

Procedure

Ask the children to sort the coins into the treasure chest and the waste bin, putting the coins with proper words on them (e.g. win) in the treasure chest and those with meaningless words (e.g. jowd) in the waste bin.

Answers

Section 1: key terminology for a systematic and structured programme

Fidelity to a programme
When teaching systematic, synthetic phonics, it is important to adhere to a teaching framework that ensures that all grapheme–phoneme correspondences are taught. This does not necessarily mean that only one programme can be used. However, mixing too many elements from different programmes can result in a lack of essential coherence across a teaching framework.

Systematic progression
An effective systematic, synthetic phonics programme begins with learning grapheme–phoneme correspondences (GPCs) in a specific order. These are used to blend CVC words from the outset. Following on from that, more GPCs are taught until all 40+ phonemes are introduced. Some 'tricky words', that are complex to decode, are introduced at a pace of approx. 3–5 per week. Next, alternative pronunciations and

spellings for graphemes are taught. Application of GPCs taught in reading and writing is provided throughout.

Criteria for assuring high-quality phonic work

The DfE provides schools with criteria which define the key features of an effective, systematic, synthetic phonics programme. Published programmes should meet each of the criteria. This can be accessed at **http://www.education.gov.uk/schools/teachingandlearning/pedagogy/a0010240/criteria-for-assuring-high-quality-phonic-work**.

Section 2: criteria for assuring high-quality phonic work

You were asked to select which of the following are included in the DfE core criteria for assuring high-quality phonic work that identifies the key features of an effective, systematic, synthetic phonics programme. You were also asked to consider a rationale for your choices.

1. Include a variety of ready-made resources.	No – whilst this might be desirable, it is not an essential criteria.
2. Teach children to blend phonemes, in order, all through a word to read it.	Yes – it is essential for children to learn the skill of blending phonemes, all through a word, from the outset.
3. Teach children to remember all words by sight.	No – children should use their knowledge of GPCs and the skill of blending to read words.
4. Introduced one grapheme–phoneme correspondence a week.	No – when learning new GPCs, this should be at a pace of between 3 and 5 a week, depending on the phase children are working in.
5. Teach actions for each grapheme–phoneme correspondence, to help children to remember them.	No – whilst some programmes use this approach, it is not an essential criterion. There are other ways children can learn the GPCs (e.g. through mnemonics).
6. Teach all 40+ grapheme–phoneme correspondences in a clear, incremental sequence.	Yes – this is essential to ensure that GPCs are not missed out and children have an opportunity to revisit, review and apply GPCs that have been taught.
7. Teach children a range of different strategies for working out an unknown word – e.g. looking at the picture, using the context of what has been read so far, thinking about what would make sense in the complete sentence.	No – children should use their knowledge of phonics as the prime approach to working out unknown words. Other strategies encourage them to guess a word, rather than work it out. This often leads to guessing an incorrect word.
8. Be designed to deliver discrete daily phonics session.	Yes – as this allows suitable attention to be given to securing word recognition skills. Phonics should be viewed as a body of knowledge to be taught rather than a strategy. Although opportunities should be sought to allow children to apply aspects of phonic knowledge and skills throughout the curriculum.
9. Allow children to apply their knowledge of grapheme–phoneme correspondences by reading texts which are entirely decodable.	Yes – reading decodable texts provides essential practice in reading known phonemes and blending and increases confidence. This should form part of children's reading diet and should not preclude other reading such as children's favourite books.
10. Be designed to ensure that the vast majority of children have secured word recognition skills by the end of Key Stage 1.	Yes – children should have secure phonic knowledge and skills which allow them to be fluent readers and confident writers by the age of seven.

Section 3: pace and progression

You were asked to match the statements in the second column with the correct phase, based on the expected length of time spent teaching it and to which year group:

Phase from Letters and Sounds	Expected length of time to be spent teaching this phase and to which year group
Phase 1	From Nursery and throughout all phases
Phase 2	Up to 6 weeks – Reception
Phase 3	Up to 12 weeks – end of Reception
Phase 4	4–6 weeks – Year 1
Phase 5	Throughout Year 1
Phase 6	Throughout Year 2

Section 4: a systematic structured approach

You were asked to use the table, taken from *Letters and Sounds*, to decide which phase each of the activities belongs to. You were also asked to consider a rationale, based on the knowledge and skills each is designed to teach.

Activity	Phase from *Letters and Sounds*	Knowledge and skills the activity is designed to teach
Activity 1: what's in the box?	Phase 4	Reading words containing adjacent consonants by blending phonemes all through the word.
Activity 2: what's missing?	Phase 2	Learn to blend phonemes all through the word to read CVC words.
Activity 3: phoneme frame	Phase 6	Reinforce understanding and application of the -*ed* suffix for the past tense.
Activity 4: quick copy	Phase 5	Recognise two-letter and three-letter graphemes in words and not read them as individual letters.
Activity 5: buried treasure	Phase 3	Practise blending GPCs that have been taught to read words.

What to do next?

Reinforce your knowledge and understanding of teaching a systematic and structured programme by doing as many as possible of the following:

• Ask teachers which phonics programme is used in their schools, and use the criteria for assuring high-quality phonic work to find out about its key features and how it is used.

- Read Chapter 9 in *Teaching Systematic Synthetic Phonics in Primary Schools* (Jolliffe *et al.*, 2012) to find out more about systematic, synthetic phonics programmes and theoretical perspectives.

- Observe a phonics lesson and consider what phonics skills and knowledge are being taught and how it fits in with a systematic approach.

Websites

There are several useful websites where you can find information about the criteria for assuring high-quality phonics work and systematic, synthetic phonics programmes. These include:

Criteria for assuring high-quality phonic work (**http://www.education. gov.uk/schools/teachingandlearning/pedagogy/a0010240/ criteria-for-assuring-high-quality-phonic-work**).

Guidance for practitioners on planning the daily discrete teaching sessions for phonics (**http://www.teachfind.com/national-strategies/planning-week-discrete- teaching-phonics-and-further-application-across-curriculum**).

Publishers of systematic, synthetic phonics programmes self-assessment against the criteria for assuring high-quality phonic work (**http://www. education.gov.uk/schools/teachingandlearning/pedagogy/b00198579/ phonics-products-and-the-self-assessment-process**).

Recommended reading

DCSF (2007) *Letters and Sounds: principles and practice of high quality phonics*. London: DCSF.

Johnston, R. and Watson, J. (2007) *Teaching Synthetic Phonics*. London: Learning Matters/SAGE.

Jolliffe, W. and Waugh, D. with Carss, A. (2012) *Teaching Systematic Synthetic Phonics in Primary Schools*. London: Learning Matters/SAGE (Chapter 9).

10 Planning for phonics

Work through each section below, responding to each question or task. When you have completed each section, you can read the answers at the end of the chapter. At the end of this chapter you can also find support for further reading and study related to planning for phonics.

Section 1: key terminology for planning for phonics

Provide a generic description for what you might include in each section of a phonics lesson as listed below:

- revisit and review

- teach

- practise

- apply

Section 2: a teaching sequence

Jolliffe *et al.* (2012: 119) state that:

> *Phonics planning should include and address:*
>
> *the four elements of a well-structured phonics session – revisit and review, teach, practise and apply;*
>
> *activities to teach and support blending for reading and segmenting for spelling;*
>
> *opportunities to learn and practise high-frequency words, tricky words, phonemes and graphemes;*
>
> *continual assessment of children's knowledge and ability.*

Analyse the sample lesson plan below to identify where any of the above are addressed:

Synthetic phonics daily plan

Phase	*Letters and Sounds* - **phase three.**
Resources	Letter cards *i, e, m, o, f, n, l, k, h, g, p* from phase two.
	sh card.
	Word cards – some with *sh* some without but using phonemes already known.
	Silly questions.
Daily discrete teaching session	
Introduction	We are learning:
	the phoneme *sh*.
	to blend phonemes including the *sh* phoneme to help us to read.
Revisit and review recently and previously learned GPCs	First let us see if we can remember the phonemes from phase two:
	Revisit *i, e, m, o, f, n, l, k, h, g, p* from phase two.
	Hold up the card with the grapheme on and children say the phoneme.
	Repeat but this time play 'mood sounds' where children have to say a phoneme in a particular way – e.g. in a happy, sad, grumpy mood etc…
Teach new GPCs	*Hear it and say it*
	Say the phoneme with its action (e.g. putting your fingers to your lips as though quietening everyone).
	Invite the children to join in.
	If any children in the room have names that contain the /sh/ phoneme, say their names, accentuating the *shhhhh* (e.g. Shhhona, Mishhha). If Charlene offers her name, accept it and leave the explanation of the letters until 'See it and say it' below. Do the same with other words (e.g. *shhheep, bushhh*), accepting suggestions from the children if they offer them.
	See it and say it
	Display *sh* and explain that this phoneme needs two letters that the children already know, and that to show that two letters stand for one phoneme we draw a line under them. (Now is the time to tell Charlene that her name certainly does start with /sh/ but that it has a different spelling.)
	Recall that the children have already seen two letters being used in the recently learned *ck* and the double letters *ll, zz, ff* and *ss* at the ends of some words.
Practise	All children stand up. Give out words to pairs of children (some contain *sh* and some don't). Ask pairs to see if their word has a *sh* in it. If it has, jump on the spot or clap hands or hop etc… Muddle cards and repeat two or three times. The last time, sound the words out and blend them to read the words. Children put thumbs up when they hear the /sh/ phoneme.
Apply their phonics learning while reading/ writing	Play yes/no questions. Show the questions below. Allow time for the children to read them and to stand up if the answer is *yes* and stay sitting if it is *no*:
	Are fish and chips food?
	Can we get wool from sheep?
	Will all shops sell nails?
	Are the teeth of sharks sharp?
	Can we see fish in rivers?
	Will a ship sail on a road?

Phase	*Letters and Sounds* - **phase three.**
	After each question, choose a pair of children to read it together and check the answers.
	Have we learned the phoneme /sh/?
	Show *sh* card. What phoneme does it represent? In pairs, can you think of a word that contains the /sh/ phoneme?
	Are we able to blend phonemes to read words with the /sh/ phoneme in them?
	Show words containing /sh/ phoneme (*ship, shark, shop, fish, shell, shed, wish, dish*). How quickly can children read them?

Note: this is based on the *Letters and Sounds* suggested daily sequence. If your school uses a different phonics programme, you may want to use the school's planning proforma.

Answers

Section 1: key terminology for planning for phonics

You were asked to provide a generic description for what might be include in each section of a phonics lesson as listed below. You might have also included specific activities.

Revisit and review

Revise previous teaching and learning. In this section of the lesson you might include revising an element that children had difficulties with in a prior lesson. It is likely you would include a re-cap of learning in the current phase or the previous phase.

Teach

Provide opportunities to teach new tricky words and/or GPCs. You might also use this element of the session to teach new concepts and skills or new games and activities.

Practise

Often through playing a range of enjoyable and interactive games, this element provides opportunities for children to consolidate their learning. You may use games to practise blending for reading or segmenting for spelling skills as well as practising the new learning from the teach element.

Apply

Provide opportunities for children to apply new and prior learning through reading and/or writing. You might do this through playing games or through reading and/ or writing sentences. You will also use this element of the lesson to assess whether the learning outcomes have been achieved and what you may need to include in the revisit and review for the next lesson.

Section 2: a teaching sequence

You were asked to analyse the sample lesson plan to identify any of the key features to be included and addressed in phonics planning, as stated by Jolliffe *et al*. (2012). You may have noted additional elements too.

Synthetic phonics daily plan

		Commentary
Introduction	We are learning: the phoneme *sh*. to blend phonemes including the *sh* phoneme to help us to read.	The learning objective is clear and shared with the children. This facilitates assessment by the teacher and self-assessment by the children.
Revisit and review recently and previously learned GPCs	First let us see if we can remember the phonemes from phase two: Revisit *i, e, m, o, f, n, l, k, h, g, p* from phase two. Hold up the card with the grapheme on and children say the phoneme. Repeat but this time play 'mood sounds' where children have to say a phoneme in a particular way – e.g. in a happy, sad, grumpy mood etc…	Opportunities to practise GPCs already learned. Assessment opportunity: the teacher can identify any children who provide an incorrect phoneme for the grapheme.
Teach new GPCs	***Hear it and say it*** Say the phoneme with its action (e.g. putting your fingers to your lips as though quietening everyone). Invite the children to join in. If any children in the room have names that contain the *sh* phoneme, say their names, accentuating the *shhhhh* (e.g. Shhhona, Mishhha). If Charlene offers her name, accept it and leave the explanation of the letters until 'See it and say it' below. Do the same with other words (e.g. *shhheep, bushhh*), accepting suggestions from the children if they offer them. ***See it and say it*** Display *sh* and explain that this phoneme needs two letters that the children already know and that to show that two letters stand for one phoneme we draw a line under them. (Now is the time to tell Charlene that her name certainly does start with /sh/ but that it has a different spelling.) Recall that the children have already seen two letters being used in the recently learned *ck* and the double letters *ll, zz, ff* and *ss* at the ends of some words.	Opportunity to learn a new GPC. Preparing for future learning. Relating new learning to prior learning.

		Commentary
Practise	All children stand up. Give out words to pairs of children (some contain *sh* and some don't). Ask pairs to see if their word has a *sh* in it. If it has jump on the spot or clap hands or hop etc… Muddle cards and repeat two or three times. The last time sound the words out and blend them to read the words. Children put thumbs up when they hear the *sh* phoneme.	This activity teaches and supports blending for reading.
Apply their phonics learning while reading/writing	Play yes/no questions. Show the questions below. Allow time for the children to read them and stand up if the answer is yes and stay sitting if it is no: • Are fish and chips food? • Can we get wool from sheep? • Will all shops sell nails? • Are the teeth of sharks sharp? • Can we see fish in rivers? • Will a ship sail on a road? After each question choose a pair of children to read it together and check the answers. Have we learned the phoneme *sh*? Show *sh* card. What phoneme does it represent? In pairs, can you think of a word that contains the *sh* phoneme? Are we able to blend phonemes to read words with the *sh* phoneme in them? Show words containing the *sh* phoneme (ship, shark, shop, fish, shell, shed, wish, dish). How quickly can children read them?	This activity allows the children to apply their knowledge of blending phonemes, in order to read a short sentence. It also reinforces the new GPC that has been taught. Assessment opportunity: the teacher can identify children who have difficulty in reading the question in pairs and note which words or GPCs that they are having difficulty with. Assessment opportunity: the teacher can check whether the children can apply their knowledge of the new GPC by providing a word that contains it. Assessment opportunity: the teacher checks whether the children can use the new GPC when sounding out and blending to read words containing it.

What to do next?

Reinforce your knowledge and understanding of planning for phonics by doing as many as possible of the following:

• Ask to look at phonics planning used by a range of different teachers, note where any of the key features discussed in this chapter are evident or, even better, discuss the planning with the teacher.

• Read Chapter 10 in *Teaching Systematic Synthetic Phonics in Primary Schools* (Jolliffe *et al.*, 2012) to find out more about a rationale for the structure of an effective phonics lesson and the key features to include.

• Observe a phonics lesson and note whether the structure follows the four-part structure. Discuss your observations with the teacher afterwards.

Websites

There are several useful websites where you can find examples of phonics lesson plans. These include:

Examples of discrete teaching at each phase in *Letters and Sounds* (**http://www. teachfind.com/national-strategies/planning-week-discrete-teaching-phonics-and-further-application-across-curriculu**).

Example plans with resources from Cambridgeshire County Council (**http://c99.e2bn. net/e2bn/leas/c99/schools/c97/accounts/pnslit/Homepage%202/Teaching%20 %26%20Learning/Phonics%26Spelling_folder/Phonics_Planning_page/**).

Useful planning from Babcock Education for all phases in *Letters and Sounds* (**http:// www.babcock-education.co.uk/ldp/v.asp?rootid=17&level2=391&depth=3&l evel3=1303&folderid=1303**).

Recommended reading

DCSF (2007) *Letters and Sounds: principles and practice of high quality phonics*. London: DCSF.

DCSF (2009) *Support for Spelling*. London: DCSF.

Hall, K. (2006) 'How children learn to read and how phonics helps', in M. Lewis and S. Ellis (eds) *Phonics, Practice, Research and Policy*. London: Paul Chapman (for further information on planning effective phonics lessons).

Jolliffe, W. and Waugh, D. with Carss, A. (2012) *Teaching Systematic Synthetic Phonics in Primary Schools*. London: Learning Matters/SAGE (Chapter 10).

11 Tracking and assessing pupils' learning

Learning outcomes

This chapter will help you to audit your:

- understanding of tracking and assessing pupils' learning in phonics and how this supports planning for appropriate next steps;
- understanding of a range of strategies for assessing and tracking pupils' progress.

Work through each section below, responding to each question or task. When you have completed each section, you can read the answers at the end of the chapter. At the end of this chapter you can also find support for further reading and study related to tracking and assessing pupils' learning.

Section 1: key terminology for a systematic and structured programme

It is important that you understand the terms below before you move on to the next activity. Provide a definition of each and check your definitions against those at the end of the chapter:

- formative assessment

- diagnostic assessment

- tracking pupil progress

- over-learning

- pseudo-words

- word recognition

- language comprehension

Section 2: the Simple View of Reading

The Simple View of Reading (Figure 11.1) makes it clear that reading necessitates word recognition processes as well as language comprehension processes. Read the

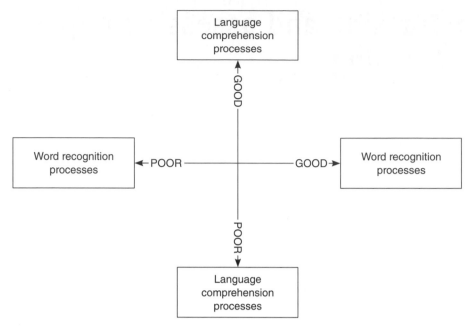

Figure 11.1   The Simple View of Reading

Source: DfES (2006: 53)

profiles of each of the four children below and decide in which quadrant each should be placed in the Simple View of Reading, based on their word recognition and language comprehension abilities. Also, consider what you could do to develop their reading skills further.

Amy does not enjoy listening to stories. She has a limited knowledge of grapheme–phoneme correspondences and finds blending to decode a challenge. She says: 'I don't like books. I can't read them and I get bored when Mr Thomas reads us stories because I get distracted.'

Harry enjoys having books read to him and he is able to talk about the content. He is not yet able to decode words for himself. He says: 'I like listening to stories and looking at books. It is hard to read them myself though.'

Richard is able to read fluently and is keen to answer questions about the content of books. Occasionally, he has difficulty with text that requires specialist knowledge. He says: 'I like reading books by Michael Morpurgo because his characters are very believable. Sometimes his books make me laugh and sometimes they make me sad.'

Harprit is able to decode words on the page but she finds it difficult to make sense of what she has read. She says: 'When we have guided reading, the other children can answer questions about the book but I find this hard.'

Section 3: assessing and tracking pupils' progress

The tracking sheet in Figure 11.1 is useful for monitoring children's progress. Children can be assessed on a half-termly basis, using the *Letters and Sounds* progress checks (DCSF, 2009: Appendix 3, pp. 197–207). If they are deemed to be secure in a phase, they are placed in the next phase on the tracking sheet.

Use the assessment information on the three children provided below, and the *Letters and Sounds* guidance on what children should be able to do to be secure in a particular phase (in Figure 11.2) to decide which phase on the tracker sheet to place each of the three children for the second half of the spring term (tinted column).

Sarah is able to segment and spell most CVC words using phase 2 and 3 graphemes. When shown a grapheme, she is able to provide the correct phoneme for the majority of phase 2 and 3 graphemes. Sarah can easily sound out and blend to read CVC words using phase 2 and 3 graphemes. She is just starting to read some words containing adjacent consonants. She has difficulty with segmenting to spell words that contain adjacent consonants.

Eden is able to use his phonic knowledge to read unfamiliar words and he is now reading both two and three-syllable words. He has a good grasp of all the GPCs that he has been taught and is able to use them in both his reading and spelling. He is confident with his use of different graphemes for long vowel phonemes and is starting to use them correctly in his spelling.

Mary has developed a good understanding of adjacent consonants and is able to read many words that contain them. She is also starting to use them when spelling words. Mary has a good grasp of all the GPCs taught in phases 2 and 3.

Are there any children who have not made any progress over the year so far?

Section 4: the Year 1 screening check

Look at each of the following statements about the Year 1 screening check and decide whether they are true or false:

1. The screening check can be done as a group assessment.

2. There is no time limit for the screening check.

3. There is a set week for schools to administer the phonics screening check.

4. Children need to read all the words correctly to reach the expected standard for the check.

Children are secure at phase 3 when they can:

- find from a display all or most phase 2 and 3 graphemes when given the sound;
- blend and read CVC words consisting of phase 2 and 3 graphemes;
- segment and make a phonemically plausible attempt at spelling CVC words using phase 2 and 3 graphemes (DCSF, 200: 15).

Children are secure at phase 4 when they can:

- give the sound when shown any phase 2 and phase 3 graphemes;
- find from a display any phase 2 and 3 grapheme when given the sound;
- blend and read words containing adjacent consonants;
- segment and spell words containing adjacent consonants (DCSF, 200: 15).

Children are secure at phase 5 when they can:

- give the sound when shown any grapheme that has been taught;
- write the common graphemes for any given sound;
- use phonic skill and knowledge as the prime approach to reading and spelling unfamiliar words, including those that are not completely decodable;
- read and spell phonically decodable two-syllable and three-syllable words (DCSF, 200: 16).

Class:
Teacher/Practitioner: 2013–2014

Progression		Autumn		Spring		Summer	
Phase 1 continuous through phase 2–6 *Show aware-ness of rhyme and alliteration. Distinguish between different sounds in the environ-ment and phonemes. Explore and experiment with sounds and words.*	**Phase 6 throughout year 2** Working on: recognising phonic irregularities and becoming more secure with less common grapheme–phoneme correspondences. Working on: applying phonic skills and knowledge to recognise and spell an increasing number of complex words. SEE SUPPORT FOR SPELLING.				*Michael Abby Heather*		**Y2**

Class: Teacher/Practitioner: 2013–2014						
Phase 5 – throughout Y1 up to 30 wks Working on: reading phonically decodable two-syllable and three-syllable words. Working on: using alternative ways of pronouncing and spelling the graphemes corresponding to the long vowel phonemes. Working on: spelling complex words using phonically plausible attempts.		Michael Abby	Michael Abby Heather Craig **Eden** Andrew Steven	Craig Andrew Steven Matthew Anne		**Y1**
Phase 4 (YR/Y1) 4–6 weeks Working on: segmenting adjacent consonants in words and apply this in spelling. Working on: blending adjacent consonants in words and applying this skill when reading unfamiliar texts.		Heather Craig Eden Abby Michael Andrew Steven	Heather Craig Eden Andrew Steven Susan Lily	Susan Lily John S Peter **Mary** Matthew Anne	Susan Lily John S Peter Rosie John R	**YR/Y1**
Phase 3 (YR) up to 12 weeks *Working on: knowing one grapheme for each of the 43 phonemes.*	Working on: reading and spelling a wide range of CVC words using all letters and less frequent consonant digraphs and some long vowel pho-nemes. Graphemes: *ear, air, ure, er ar, or, ur, ow, oi ai, ee, igh, oa, oo* *Working on: reading and spelling CVC words using a wider range of letters, short vowels, some consonant digraphs and double letters.* *Consonant digraphs:*	John S Peter Mary Lily Matthew Anne Susan Sarah Harry Rosie	John S Peter Mary Matthew Anne Sarah Harry Rosie John R	**Sarah** Harry Rosie John R Rebecca David	Rebecca David Harry	

(Continued)

(Continued)

Class: Teacher/Practitioner: 2013–2014						
	ch, sh, th, ng Working on: reading and spelling CVC words using letters and short vowels. Letter progression: Set 7: *y, z, zz, qu* Set 6: *j, v, w, x*					
	Phase 2 – up to 6 weeks Working on: using common consonants and vowels. Blending for reading and segmenting for spelling simple CVC words. Working on: knowing that words are constructed from phonemes and that phonemes are represented by graphemes. Letter progression: Set 5: *h, b, f, ff, l, ll, ss* Set 4: *ck, e, u, r* Set 3: *g, o, c, k* Set 2: *i, n, m, d* Set 1: *s, a, t, p*	John R Rebecca David	Rebecca David			
	Phase 1 (7 Aspects) throughout all phases Working on: showing awareness of rhyme and alliteration, distinguishing between different sounds in the environment and phonemes, exploring and experimenting with sounds and words and discriminating speech sounds in words. Beginning to orally blend and segment phonemes.					

Figure 11.2   Phonic progress tracking sheet – Early Years Foundation Stage through Key Stage 1

5. A teaching assistant may administer the screening check.

6. The screening check forms part of schools' statutory assessment and reporting arrangements.

7. The screening check can be stopped part way through if it is evident that the child is struggling with it.

8. All children in Year 1 must take the check, regardless of their ability in phonics.

9. If a child is absent when the test is administered, they can't do it at another time.

10. Teachers must tell parents whether or not their child has met the required standard.

11. The check must be administered to children in Year 2 if they did not take the check in Year 1 or if they did not reach the expected standard when they took the test in Year 1.

12. The screening check includes pseudo-words in order to prevent bias to those with a good vocabulary knowledge or visual memory of words.

Answers

Section 1: key terminology for a systematic and structured programme

You were asked to define each of the key terms below:

Formative assessment
Forms an integral part of teaching and learning. It contributes to learning through providing feedback and should inform future planning and next steps.

Diagnostic assessment
Assesses the nature of difficulties that a child might have.

Tracking pupil progress
Involves using assessments to identify children who may need additional support. It is also used to inform the organisation of phonic work. It is designed to make sure all children make maximum progress.

Pseudo-words
These are nonsense words which are used to assess children's ability to decode.

Word recognition
The ability to read the words on the page.

Language comprehension
The ability to understand oral and written language.

Section 2: the Simple View of Reading

You were asked to decide in which quadrant the four children should be placed in the Simple View of Reading, based on their word recognition and language comprehension abilities (see Figure 11.3). You were also asked to consider what you could do to develop their reading skills further.

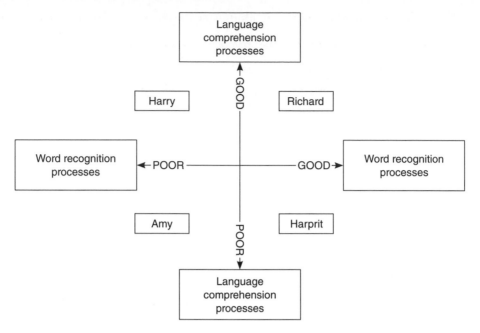

Figure 11.3 The Simple View of Reading: annotated

Source: DfES (2006: 53)

Amy has poor word recognition and poor comprehension skills.

Support needed – phonics and language immersion:

- A systematic, synthetic phonics programme.
- Experience of nursery rhymes and traditional stories.
- Developing speaking and listening skills through, for example, using a range of questioning, checking for understanding, modelling active listening and providing opportunities for group discussion.

Harry has poor word recognition skills but good comprehension skills.

Support needed:

- More work on letter/sound correspondence.
- Help with blending phonemes in order.
- Help with segmenting words into separate phonemes.
- To be shown that segmenting and blending are reversible.

Richard has good word recognition skills and good comprehension skills.

Support needed:

- Work on inference and deduction.

- Drama: e.g. role-play, hot-seating and conscience alley.

- Opportunities to read a wide range of texts.

- Reading comprehension activities.

- More work on assessing pupils' progress assessment focuses: AF3, AF4, AF5, AF6 and AF7 activities. See **http://webarchive.nationalarchives.gov. uk/20110202093118/http://nationalstrategies.standards.dcsf.gov.uk/ node/20411** for further information.

Harprit has good word recognition skills but poor comprehension skills.

Support needed:

- Work on reading retrieval/comprehension skills.

- More experience of reading comprehension activities.

- More work on assessing pupils' progress assessment focus AF2 activities. See **http://webarchive.nationalarchives.gov.uk/20110202093118/http:// nationalstrategies.standards.dcsf.gov.uk/node/20411** for further information.

Class: Teacher/Practitioner: 2013–2014							
Progression		**Autumn**		**Spring**		**Summer**	
Phase 1 continuous through phase 2–6 Show awareness of rhyme and alliteration. Distinguish between different sounds in the environment and phonemes. Explore and experiment with sounds and words.	**Phase 6 throughout Year 2** Working on: recognising phonic irregularities and becoming more secure with less common grapheme–phoneme correspondences. Working on: applying phonic skills and knowledge to recognise and spell an increasing number of complex words. SEE SUPPORT FOR SPELLING.				<u>Eden</u> Michael Abby Heather		Y2
	Phase 5 – throughout Y1 up to 30 wks Working on: reading phonically decodable two-syllable and three-syllable words. Working on: using alternative ways of pronouncing and spelling the graphemes corresponding to the long vowel phonemes. Working on: spelling complex words using phonically plausible attempts.		Michael Abby	Michael Abby Heather Craig Eden Andrew Steven	<u>Mary</u> Craig Andrew Steven Matthew Anne		Y1

(Continued)

(Continued)

Class: Teacher/Practitioner:		2013–2014				
	Phase 4 (YR/Y1) 4–6 weeks Working on: segmenting adjacent consonants in words and apply this in spelling. Working on: blending adjacent consonants in words and applying this skill when reading unfamiliar texts.	Heather Craig Eden Abby Michael Andrew Steven	Heather Craig Eden Andrew Steven Susan Lily	Susan Lily John S Peter Mary Matthew Anne	**<u>Sarah</u>** Susan Lily John S Peter Rosie John R	YR/Y1
	Phase 3 (YR) *up to 12 weeks* *Working on:* *knowing one* *grapheme for* *each of the 43* *phonemes.*	Working on: reading and spelling a wide range of CVC words using all letters and less frequent consonant digraphs and some long vowel phonemes. *Graphemes:* *ear, air, ure, er* *ar, or, ur, ow, oi* *ai, ee, igh, oa, oo* Working on: reading and spelling CVC words using a wider range of letters, short vowels, some consonant digraphs and double letters. *Consonant* *digraphs:* *ch, sh, th, ng* Working on: reading and spelling CVC words using letters and short vowels. *Letter* *progression:* *Set 7: y, z, zz, qu* *Set 6: j, v, w, x*	John S Peter Mary Lily Matthew Anne Susan Sarah Harry Rosie	John S Peter Mary Matthew Anne Sarah Harry Rosie John R	Sarah Harry Rosie John R Rebecca David	Rebecca David Harry	

Class: Teacher/Practitioner:		2013–2014					
	Phase 2 – up to 6 weeks Working on: using common consonants and vowels. Blending for reading and segmenting for spelling simple CVC words. Working on: knowing that words are constructed from phonemes and that phonemes are represented by graphemes. Letter progression: *Set 5: h, b, f, ff, l, ll, ss* *Set 4: ck, e, u, r* *Set 3: g, o, c, k* *Set 2: i, n, m, d* *Set 1: s, a, t, p*	John R Rebecca David	Rebecca David				
	Phase 1 (7 Aspects) throughout all phases Working on: showing awareness of rhyme and alliteration, distinguishing between different sounds in the environment and phonemes, exploring and experimenting with sounds and words and discriminating speech sounds in words. Beginning to orally blend and segment phonemes.						

Figure 11.4 Phonic progress tracking sheet – Early Years Foundation Stage through Key Stage 1

Section 3: assessing and tracking pupils' progress

You were asked to use the information provided on three children and the *Letters and Sounds* guidance of expectations of what to look for at each phase to decide where they should be placed on the tracking sheet for the second half of the spring term (please see the tracking sheet with the three children added shown in Figure 11.4).

You were also asked whether any children had not made any progress over the year so far. Harry has remained in phase 3 throughout the year.

Section 4: the Year 1 screening check

You were asked to look at the statements about the Year 1 screening check and decide whether they are true or false.

1.	The screening check can be done as a group assessment.	False: the check has to be carried out on an individual basis.
2.	There is no time limit for the screening check.	True: however, it is expected that the check should take between four and nine minutes for each child. It is important for children to be allowed enough time to respond to each word.
3.	There is a set week for schools to administer the phonics screening check.	True: the check can be administered on any day during the given week in June.
4.	Children need to read all the words correctly to reach the expected standard for the check.	False: each year the school will be sent the threshold mark with the screening check scoring guidance. This will state the number of words the child will need to have read correctly to reach the expected standard.
5.	A teaching assistant may administer the screening check.	False: the check must be administered by a teacher as it requires professional judgement about which responses are correct. The teacher should be known to the child but should not be a parent or relative.
6.	The screening check forms part of schools' statutory assessment and reporting arrangements.	True: all maintained schools are required to administer the check along with academies (including free schools) where it is a requirement of their funding agreement. Independent schools are not formally required to participate.
7.	The screening check can be stopped part way through if it is evident that the child is struggling with it.	True: a teacher may decide to stop the check if the child is getting distressed. If the child is showing signs of fatigue, the teacher may decide to give them a short rest break before continuing.
8.	All children in Year 1 must take the check, regardless of their ability in phonics.	False: a headteacher may decide that a child should not participate in the check but they should be reconsidered for the check the following year. The headteacher is required to explain their decision to the child's parents.
9.	If a child is absent when the test is administered, they can't do it at another time.	False: the school can administer the phonics screening check up until the Friday of the following week.
10.	Teachers must tell parents whether or not their child has met the required standard.	True: this must be done by the end of the summer term at the latest.
11.	The check must be administered to children in Year 2 if they did not take the check in Year 1 or if they did not reach the expected standard when they took the test in Year 1.	True: if a child has not reached the expected standard in Year 2, they will not need to retake the check in Year 3. Schools will be expected to provide a programme of support for these children.
12.	The screening check includes pseudo-words in order to prevent bias to those with a good vocabulary knowledge or visual memory of words.	True: these words will be new to all children and, as such, reading them will depend on their ability to use phonics decoding rather than any other strategies.

What to do next?

Reinforce your knowledge and understanding of tracking and assessment by doing as many as possible of the following:

- Observe teachers carrying out assessments of children's phonic knowledge as part of their tracking of pupils' progress.

- Read Chapter 11 in *Teaching Systematic Synthetic Phonics in Primary Schools* (Jolliffe *et al.*, 2012) to find out more about methods of assessing and tracking children's phonic knowledge and examples of intervention.

- Carry out an assessment appropriate to the phonics programme used in your school to identify a child's strengths and areas for development.

Websites

There are several useful websites where you can find information about tracking and assessing pupils' progress in phonics. These include:

Information about the phonics screening check can be found at **http://www. education.gov.uk/schools/teachingandlearning/pedagogy/phonics/a00197709/ phonics-screening-year-1**.

A phonics screening check training video can be accessed at **http://www.youtube. com/watch?v=IPJ_ZEBh1Bk**.

A range of assessment resources from Babcock Education can be found at **http://www. babcock-education.co.uk/ldp/v.asp?rootid=17&level2=391&depth=3&level3= 1303&folderid=1303**.

Recommended reading

DCSF (2007) *Letters and Sounds: principles and practice of high quality phonics*. London: DCSF.

DCSF (2009) *Phonics: assessment and tracking guidance* (Ref: 00906–2009PDF-EN-01). London: DCSF (for further guidance on tracking).

DfES (2006) *Independent Review of the Teaching of Early Reading: final report (the Rose Report)*. Nottingham: DfES (a clear rationale about the importance of ongoing assessment).

Jolliffe, W. and Waugh, D. with Carss, A. (2012) *Teaching Systematic Synthetic Phonics in Primary Schools*. London: Learning Matters/SAGE.

12 Phonics at Key Stage 2

> **Learning outcomes**
>
> This chapter will help you to audit your:
>
> - strategies for supporting those children who require additional support at Key Stage 2, using methods and resources which address pupils' learning needs but are also suitable for their maturity levels;
> - knowledge of strategies for extending the phonic knowledge and understanding of those children who are successful readers;
> - knowledge of morphology.

Work through each section below, responding to each question or task. When you have completed each section, you can read the answers at the end of the chapter. At the end of this chapter you can also find support for further reading and study related to phonics at Key Stage 2.

Section 1: key terminology for phonics at Key Stage 2

It is important that you understand the terms below before you move on to the next activity. Provide a definition of each and check your definitions against those at the end of the chapter:

- etymology
- grapheme–phoneme correspondence
- adjacent consonants
- monosyllabic words
- free morpheme
- bound morpheme
- prefix
- suffix

Section 2: exploring morphemes (see also Chapter 6)

Look at the word *friend*. Add a suffix and you can change *friend* to *friendly*, *friends*, *friendless* or *friendliness*. Add a prefix to *friend* and you can make *befriend* or even, from

Facebook, *unfriend*! By adding prefixes and suffixes you could make: *befriends*, *befriended*, *unfriendly* and *unfriendliness*.

Look at the words below and see how many words you can create using them as root words and adding affixes (prefixes and or suffixes):

- help

- like

- play

Section 3: meanings of morphemes

Look at the list of prefixes below and the words next to them and provide a definition for each prefix:

- *un-*   unusual

- *bi-*   bicycle

- *re-*   reuse

- *anti-*   antifreeze

- *sub-*   subway

Notice how the spellings of prefixes tend to be phonically regular. How can learning about prefixes help children with reading and spelling? NB Many teachers don't tend to segment or use sound buttons on morphemes, as this shifts the focus from meaning to decoding.

Section 4: segmenting words into morphemes (see also Chapter 6)

Look at the words below and segment them into morphemes (for example, delighted – de/light/ed). Morphemes which can stand alone as words are called free morphemes. Those which cannot stand alone as words are called bound morphemes. For each word, identify the free and the bound morphemes. For example, de/light/ed – de and –ed are bound morphemes; light is a free morpheme.

- exported

- prepacked

- defused

Section 5: modifying words (see also Chapter 6)

Look at the word list of spellings which Years 5 and 6 should be able to spell, according to the draft National Curriculum, and ensure that you feel confident that you can spell them all.

How many words can **not** be modified using affixes? For example, accommodate can be made into accommodates, accommodated, accommodation and accommodating; debate can be made into debates, debatable, debated, debating; favour into disfavour, unfavoured, favourable etc.

Now try to provide **one** modification for each of the words. You don't need to write down all the possible modified words for each word, but it may be useful to do this if you are teaching Years 5–6 and want to prepare for spelling lessons.

accommodate	knuckle	phrase	deprive	suggest	whether
debate	magazine	popular	foreign	vocabulary	engineer
favour	majesty	prefer	impress	bargain	interview
identify	majority	privilege	lenient	embarrass	resemble
lawyer	manage	pronunciation	statue	germ	syrup
narrate	manufacture	protect	variety (root	influence	wisdom
qualify	marvellous	punctual	*vary*)	suit	career
similar	medium	query	atmosphere	volcano	enrol
umpire	military	rapid	destroy	believe	harass
affection	mineral	realise	forty	emigrate	introduce
deceive	minor	receipt	imprison	govern(ment)	resign
familiar	miracle	recent	lightning	inhabitant	wizard
illustrate	mischief	recommend	stubborn	superior	celebrate
lecture	mischievous	refuse	attitude	volume	envelope
nation	modern	regret	develop	blemish	haughty
quench	modest	relevant	fruit	encounter	restore
sincere	moisture	imagine	include	gradual	talent
unite	mosquito	legend	liquid	instrument	woollen
analyse	natural	society	style	surprise	century
decimal	ninth	utter	ventilate	boundary	equator
festival	nuisance	ancient	average	encourage	haunt
investigate	persevere	definite	index	granite	revise
jealous	object	flavour	succeed	interfere	telescope
juice	reason	imitate	villain	remove	wrench
junction	observe	leisure	awkward	syllable	challenge
jury	occupy	solemn	garage	wardrobe	equip
knead	receive	apparent	industry	bruise	hearty
parallel	omit	demonstrate	success	endure	rhyme
permanent	operate	forbid	virtue	guarantee	tempt
vacant	opinion	sphere	electric	interrupt	committee
appreciate	organise	Europe	genuine	request	especially
rhythm	origin	European	inferior	sympathy	height
terminate	theatre	hoax	honour	purpose	twelfth
yacht	yeast	tomorrow	satisfy	saucepan	exceed
convince	correspond	parliament	tremendous	triumph	hurricane
estimate	hindrance	tyrant	zone	zoology	seize
hinder	thorough	create	curious	excavate	explanation
ridiculous	coward	zero	exaggerate	humility	severe
immense	sandwich	evidence	horizon sign	scheme	length

Look at the words again and identify the those which include 'tricky' bits which you may need to help children focus on when they learn them.

Section 6: poetry and exploring rhyming words

Look at the limerick below. Your task is to write a final line, but first look at the rhyming couplets: York and talk, and speak and week.

There was a young lady from York,

Who seemed to do nothing but talk.

When she started to speak,

It seemed like a week,

Find rhymes for York and talk and make two lists: one under York to include words which rhyme with York and have similar spellings (e.g. pork), and one under talk with words which rhyme and have similar spellings. Add other lists for other words which rhyme but have a different spelling of the rhyme. Once you have made your lists and checked any unfamiliar words in a dictionary, complete the limerick.

What do your lists tell you about possible spellings of words which rhyme with York and talk? Are there other spellings for the rhyme?

Next look at speak and week. Make lists of rhymes under the headings speak and week. How many words can you write under each in two minutes? What do your lists tell you about possible spellings of words which rhyme with speak and week? Are there other spellings for the *-eek/eak* rhyme?

Section 7: exploring activities for Key Stage 2

Children at Key Stage 2 may still need to develop their phonological awareness, but may be put off doing so if the activities and materials they are given are felt to be beneath their maturity level. It is therefore important to devise activities which engage and interest them while helping them to learn. Look at the list of football teams below and consider how you might use them to develop activities to foster phonological awareness:

Manchester United	*Chelsea*	*Rochdale*	*Doncaster Rovers*
Sunderland	*Liverpool*	*Blackpool*	*West Ham*

Answers

Section 1: key terminology for phonics at Key Stage 2

Etymology
The origins of the formation of a word and its meaning.

Grapheme–phoneme correspondence

The relationship between letters and sounds. The graphemes (letters and combinations of letters such as digraphs and trigraphs) are the written representation on the phonemes (sounds) in words.

Adjacent consonants

Consonants which appear next to each other in a word and can be blended together – e.g. *bl* in blip, *cr* in crack (note that the *ck* in crack is a digraph, as the consonants come together to form a single sound or phoneme).

Monosyllabic words

Words with one syllable – for example, book, dig, run, hot.

Free morpheme

A morpheme which can stand alone as a word – for example, in kicked, *kick* is a free morpheme, but *-ed* is a bound morpheme because it cannot stand alone – it needs to be bound to a word to have meaning.

Bound morpheme

A morpheme which cannot stand alone (see free morpheme).

Prefix

A morpheme or affix placed before a word to modify its meaning – e.g. *dis-* in dislike, *de-* in defrost.

Suffix

Morpheme or affix added to a word to modify its meaning – e.g. *-ful* in hopeful, *-ed* in jumped.

Section 2: exploring morphemes

You were asked to look at the words below and see how many words you can create using them as root words and adding affixes (prefixes and or suffixes):

- *help* could become *helpful, helpless, helps, helping, helped, helper, unhelpful* etc

- *like* could become *likeable, likes, liked, likely, likeness, liking, unlikely, unlikeable, dislike, disliking* etc

- *play* could become *playing, played, plays, playful, player, display, replay, unplayable, replaying, replayed, displayed* etc

Section 3: meanings of morphemes

You were asked to provide a definition for each prefix:

- *un-*   not

- *bi-*   two

- *re-*   again

- *anti-* against

- *sub-* under

Section 4: segmenting words into morphemes

You were asked to look at the words below and segment them into morphemes. For each word, you had to identify the free and the bound morphemes:

- exported ex/port/ed – *ex-* and *-ed* are bound morphemes; *port* (carry) is a free morpheme

- prepacked: pre/pack/ed – *pre-* and *-ed* are bound morphemes; *pack* is a free morpheme

- defused: de/fuse/ing (the *e* is dropped from *fuse* when *-ing* is added) – *de-* and *-ing* are bound morphemes; *fuse* (blend/join) is a free morpheme

NB The suffix *-ed* can have different sounds. For example, in *walked* and *danced* it has a *t* sound; while in *blessed*, *shouted* and *hated* has an *-ed* sound, and in *jogged*, *rained* and *showed* it has a *d* sound.

Section 5: modifying words

You were asked to look at the word list of spellings which Years 5 and 6 should be able to spell according to the draft National Curriculum, and ensure that you feel confident that you can spell them all. You were then asked how many words can **not** be modified using affixes. *Whether*, *lightning* and *especially* are the only words which cannot be modified.

You were then asked to try to provide **one** modification for each of the words. We have provided the list again below but with each word modified. For many words there are several possible modifications and your choices do not have to be the same as ours.

accommodated	knuckles	phrased	deprivation	suggestion	**whether**
debates	magazines	popularity	foreigner	vocabularies	engineering
favoured	majestic	preference	impressive	bargained	interviewee
identification	majorities	privileged	leniency	embarrassing	resembled
lawyers	manager	pronunciations	statue	germs	syrups
narrated	manufacturing	protection	varieties (root *vary*)	influenced	wisdoms
qualification	marvellously	punctually		suits	careers
similarity	mediums	queries	atmospheric	volcanoes	enrolment
umpiring	militaristic	rapidly	destroyed	believer	harassed
affectionate	minerals	realisation	forties	emigrated	introduced
deceived	minority	receipts	imprisoned	governmental	resigned
familiarity	miracles	recently	**lightning**	inhabitants	wizardry
illustrator	mischievous	recommended	stubbornness	superiority	celebrated
lecturing	mischievously	refusal	attitudes	volumes	enveloped
national	modernise	regrets	development	blemishes	haughtiness
quenched	modesty	relevance	fruition	encountered	restoration

insincere	moisturise	imagination	included	gradually	talented
united	mosquitoes	legendary	liquids	instrumental	woollens
analysed	naturally	societies	styles	surprised	centuries
decimalise	ninthly	utterance	ventilation	boundaries	equatorial
festivals	nuisances	anciently	averages	encouraged	haunted
investigated	perseverance	definitely	indexes	granites	revision
jealousy	objection	flavour	(indices)	interference	telescopes
juices	reasonable	imitation	succeeded	removal	wrenched
conjunction	observer	leisurely	villainous	syllables	challenged
juries	occupation	solemnly	awkwardly	wardrobes	equipment
kneaded	received	apparently	garages	bruised	heartily
parallels	omission	demonstrated	industrial	endurance	rhymed
permanently	operated	forbids	successor	guarantees	tempted
vacantly	opinionated	spherical	virtues	interruption	committees
appreciated	organisation	European	electrical	requested	**especially**
rhythmic	original	Europeans	genuineness	sympathetic	heights
terminated	theatrical	hoaxes	inferiority	purposeful	twelfths
yachts	yeasts	tomorrows	honourable	saucepans	exceeding
convinced	correspondence	parliamentary	satisfaction	triumphant	hurricanes
estimated	hindrances	tyrants	tremendously	zoological	seizure
hindered	thoroughly	creator	zones	excavated	explanations
ridiculously	cowardly	zeroes	curiously	humilities	severity
immensely	sandwiches	evidenced	exaggerated	schematic	lengthen
			horizontal		
			signal		

You were asked to look at the words again and identify those which include 'tricky' bits which you may need to help children focus on when they learn them:

- Some words lose letters when a suffix is added – for example, hinder becomes hindrance.

- Some change some letters – for example, vacant becomes vacancy, deceive becomes deception.

- Some words change the way they are pronounced when a suffix is added – for example, sign to signal; prefer to preference; severe to severity.

When you teach children about these spelling conventions, use the opportunity to show how they work for other words which they are likely to encounter:

- Some of unusual combinations of letters representing familiar sounds – for example, yacht, rhythmic, rhymed, foreigner.

- Some have double letters which can be missed – for example, accommodated, recommended, woollens, embarrassing.

- In some, the endings can be confused with other endings with similar sounds – for example, creator, successor.

- There are silent or not usually pronounced letters in some – for example, governmental, kneaded, knuckles.

There are many other potential tricky bits in many of the words. When you are planning to teach them to children, it can be a good idea to ask someone to try to spell a selection and to see which bits they find the most challenging.

Section 6: poetry and exploring rhyming words

There was a young lady from York,

Who seemed to do nothing but talk.

When she started to speak,

It seemed like a week,

You were asked to find rhymes for York and talk and make two lists: one under York to include words which rhyme with York and have similar spellings (e.g. pork) and one under talk with words which rhyme and have similar spellings. You were also asked to add other lists for other words which rhyme but have a different spelling of the rhyme.

Some suggestions:

York	talk	hawk	torque	baulk
cork fork pork	chalk walk	squawk		caulk

Once you had made your lists and checked any unfamiliar words in a dictionary, you were asked to complete the limerick.

A suggestion:

There was a young lady from York,

Who seemed to do nothing but talk.

When she started to speak,

It seemed like a week,

Of nothing but squawk, squawk and squawk.

You were asked what your lists told you about possible spellings of words which rhyme with York and talk, and if there were other spellings for the rhyme. The lists suggest that the most common way of writing the rhyme is *ork*, followed by *alk*. Other possibilities are rare.

Next you looked at speak and week and made lists of rhymes under the headings speak and week. You were asked to see how many words you could write under each in two minutes. You were asked what your lists told you about possible spellings of words which rhyme with speak and week. You were asked if there were other spellings for the *-eek/eak* rhyme.

Some suggestions:

speak	week	clique	shriek
weak	cheek	boutique	
creak	peek	antique	
freak	seek	unique	
beak	meek	technique	
pea	leek		

Section 7: exploring activities for Key Stage 2

Children at Key Stage 2 may still need to develop their phonological awareness, but may be put off doing so if the activities and materials they are given are felt to be beneath their maturity level. It is therefore important to devise activities which engage and interest them while helping them to learn. You were asked to look at the list of football teams below and consider how you might use them to develop activities to foster phonological awareness:

Manchester United   Chelsea   Rochdale   Doncaster Rovers

Sunderland   Liverpool   Blackpool   West Ham

There are many different activities you might develop using football teams or other names which are of particular interest to children. For example, you could ask children to find football matches by pairing teams which have graphemes in common – for example:

Man*ch*ester United v *Ch*elsea

*Ch*elsea v Ro*ch*dale

Doncast*er* Rov*er*s v Sund*er*land

Liver*pool* v Black*pool*

You could ask them to create matches based only on initial and final sounds – for example:

West Ha*m* v *M*anchester United

Rochda*le* v *L*iverpool

You could ask children to look at league tables to find teams which could play against teams from the group of eight above, using different criteria for pairings.

You could ask children to find names of teams which include:

- vowel digraphs (Leeds)

- consonant digraphs (Notts County, Hull)

- consonant clusters (Fleetwood, Blackburn, Leicester, Bristol City)

- trigraphs (Brighton, Bournemouth)

- quadgraphs (Middlesbrough)

- silent letters (Carlisle, Wycombe)

You could go on to give children common words and ask them to match them with football team cards where they share a sound or grapheme.

What to do next?

Reinforce your knowledge and understanding of decoding by doing as many as possible of the following:

- Observe phonics lessons at Key Stage 2.

- Build up a bank of resources which will engage children at their maturity level while helping them to develop their phonic knowledge and understanding.

- Look for poems and songs which can stimulate children's interest in rhyme and vocabulary.

Websites

There are several useful websites, including:

Grammar.yourdictionary.com – the 100 most commonly misspelled words (http:// grammar.yourdictionary.com/spelling-and-word-lists/misspelled.html).

Merriam-Webster Online Dictionary with audio pronunciations (http://www.merriam-webster.com/dictionary/).

Recommended reading

DCSF (2007) *Letters and Sounds: principles and practice of high quality phonics*. London: DCSF.

DCSF (2009) *Support for Spelling*. London: DCSF.

Johnston, R. and Watson, J. (2007) *Teaching Synthetic Phonics*. London: Learning Matters/SAGE.

Jolliffe, W. (2006) *Phonics: a complete synthetic programme*. Leamington Spa: Scholastic.

Jolliffe, W. (2007) *You Can Teach Synthetic Phonics*. Leamington Spa: Scholastic.

Jolliffe, W. and Waugh, D. with Carss, A. (2012) *Teaching Systematic Synthetic Phonics in Primary Schools*. London: Learning Matters/SAGE (Chapter 12).

13 Using a range of programmes and resources

Learning outcomes

....

This chapter will help you to audit your:

- knowledge of the most frequently-used systematic synthetic phonics programmes;
- awareness of the challenges you will face as you work with different systematic synthetic phonics programmes.

Work through each section below, responding to each question or task. When you have completed each section, you can read the answers at the end of the chapter. At the end of this chapter you can also find support for further reading and study related to using a range of programmes and resources.

Section 1: key terminology for using a range of programmes and resources

It is important that you understand the terms below before you move on to the next activity. Provide a definition of each and check your definitions against those at the end of the chapter:

- phonics first and fast

- discrete daily sessions

- fidelity to the teaching framework

- decodable texts

- phases

- core criteria

You also need to know something about each of the major phonics programmes used in schools in England. Find out as much as you can about each and note some key features. Web links have been provided to help you:

- Floppy's Phonics (**http://www.oup.com/oxed/primary/oxfordreadingtree/ resources/floppysphonics/soundsandletters/**).

- Jolly Phonics (**http://jollylearning.co.uk/overview-about-jolly-phonics/**).

- Letters and Sounds (**https://www.gov.uk/government/uploads/system/ uploads/attachment_data/file/190599/Letters_and_Sounds_-_DFES-00281- 2007.pdf**).

- Phonics Bug (**http://www.pearsonphonics.co.uk/PhonicsBug/PhonicsBug. aspx**).

- Read Write Inc. (**http://www.ruthmiskintraining.com/read-write-inc- programmes/index.html**).

- Sounds Write (**http://www.sounds-write.co.uk/**).

Section 2: criteria for successful systematic synthetic phonics programmes

What do you consider are the key features of successful phonics programmes? Look at Ofsted's (2010) *Reading by Six* report to find out the inspectorate's views (see answers section for an extract and the end of the chapter for a web link).

Before you look at the answers, think about the following:

- word recognition

- assessment

- progression

- teaching methods

- high-frequency words

Section 3: programme quiz

Which programme is being described?

- There are actions for each phoneme.

- It has a chart of speed sounds.

- There are six phases, the first of which only involves oral work.

- It is based upon *Letters and Sounds* and has a range of books, some of which can be used interactively for teaching.

- It uses an alphabetic code chart.

- There is a mnemonic to go with each grapheme–phoneme correspondence, for example, *Maisie's Mountain* and *poo at the zoo*, *cup of tea for ea*, *what can you see?* (for *ee*).

- The first five letter sound correspondences are *s a t i p*.

- The first eight letter sound correspondences are *s a t p i n m d*.

- The first ten letter sound correspondences are *m a s d t i n p g o*.

- This programme claims to teach everything children need for the DfE's Year 1 Phonics Screening Check.

In the answers section you will find charts showing the sequence of grapheme–phoneme correspondences for each of Jolly Phonics, Letters and Sounds, and Read Write Inc.

Section 4: what to look for when you meet a new programme

Now think about what you would need to find out if you found you were going to work in a school with a phonics programme you had not met before. Make a list of things to ask.

Answers

Section 1: key terminology for using a range of programmes and resources

Phonics first and fast
Children learn to apply phonic knowledge and skills as their first approach to reading and spelling. They do this as part of a systematic programme which is time-limited – for example, Letters and Sounds' six phases should normally be completed within Key Stage 1.

Discrete daily sessions
Daily sessions which focus on phonics give teachers regular opportunities to deliver high-quality phonics teaching which is not overshadowed by other subject matter.

Fidelity to the teaching framework
Fidelity to a framework or structure that ensures that all the 40+ phonemes and their alternative spellings and pronunciations are taught and applied in reading and writing. The core criteria (DfE, 2011) do not state that this should necessarily be restricted to a specific programme.

Decodable texts
Texts which have a high proportion of words which can be decoded (read) using phonic strategies.

Phases

These are stages in a systematic programme through which children progress. For example, Letters and Sounds has six phases.

Core criteria

These are set out in the DfE website and provide clearly defined key features of an effective, systematic, synthetic phonics programme.

Section 2: criteria for successful systematic synthetic phonics programmes

Ofsted's *Reading by Six* report (2010: 42) maintained that programmes for phonic work should meet each of the following criteria:

- *present high-quality systematic, synthetic phonic work as the prime approach to decoding print, i.e. a phonics 'first and fast' approach*

- *enable children to start learning phonic knowledge and skills using a systematic, synthetic programme by the age of five, with the expectation that they will be fluent readers having secure word recognition skills by the end of key stage one*

- *be designed for the teaching of discrete, daily sessions progressing from simple to more complex phonic knowledge and skills and covering the major grapheme/phoneme correspondences*

- *enable children's progress to be assessed*

- *use a multi-sensory approach so that children learn variously from simultaneous visual, auditory and kinaesthetic activities which are designed to secure essential phonic knowledge and skills*

- *demonstrate that phonemes should be blended, in order, from left to right, 'all through the word' for reading*

- *demonstrate how words can be segmented into their constituent phonemes for spelling and that this is the reverse of blending phonemes to read words*

- *ensure children apply phonic knowledge and skills as their first approach to reading and spelling, even if a word is not completely phonically regular*

- *ensure that children are taught high frequency words that do not conform completely to grapheme/phoneme correspondence rules*

- *provide fidelity to the teaching framework for the duration of the programme, to ensure that these irregular words are fully learnt*

- *ensure that as pupils move through the early stages of acquiring phonics, they are invited to practise by reading texts which are entirely decodable for them, so that they experience success and learn to rely on phonemic strategies.*

Section 3: Programme quiz

You were asked which programme was being described:

- There are actions for each phoneme (Jolly Phonics).

- It has a chart of speed sounds (Read Write Inc.).

- There are six phases, the first of which only involves oral work (Letters and Sounds).

- It is based upon *Letters and Sounds* and has a range of books, some of which can be used interactively for teaching (Phonics Bug).

- It uses an alphabetic code chart (Floppy's Phonics).

- There is a mnemonic to go with each grapheme–phoneme correspondence, for example, *Maisie's Mountain* and *poo at the zoo, cup of tea for ea, what can you see?* (for *ee*) (Read Write Inc.).

- The first five letter sound correspondences are *s a t i p* (Jolly Phonics and Letters and Sounds).

- The first eight letter sound correspondences are *s a t p i n m d* (Letters and Sounds).

- The first ten letter sound correspondences are *m a s d t i n p g o* (Read Write Inc.).

- This programme claims to teach everything children need for the DfE's Year 1 Phonics Screening Check (SoundsWrite).

Below you will find charts showing the sequence of grapheme–phoneme correspondences for each of Jolly Phonics, Letters and Sounds, and Read Write Inc.:

Jolly Phonics	*Week*
s a t i p	1
n c/k e h r	2
m d g o u	3
l f b ai j	4
oa ie ee or z w	5
ng v oo **oo** y <u>x</u>	6
ch sh th **th** <u>qu</u> ou	7
oi <u>ue</u> er ar	8

Letters and Sounds	
s a t p	Phase 2 (Reception)
i n m d	
g o c k	
ck e u r	
h b f, ff l, ll ss	
j v w <u>x</u>	Phase 3 (Reception)
y z, zz <u>qu</u>	
ch, sh, th/th, ng, ai, ee, igh, oa, oo/oo, ar, or, ur, ow, oi, ear, air, ure, er*	
zh	Phase 5 (Y1)

Note: *'er' represents a schwa (uh) sound as in mother.

Read Write Inc.	Set
m a s d t	1
i n p g o	
c k u b	
f e l h sh r	
j v y w	
th z ch <u>qu</u> <u>x</u> ng <u>nk</u>	
ay ee igh ow oo *oo* ar or air ir ou oy	2
ire ear ure ea oi a-e u-e aw are ur er ow ai oa ew	3

Note: the letters underlined are not single phonemes: nk (ngk), qu (cw), x (cs), ue (yoo).

Section 4: what to look for when you meet a new programme

Among the things you might wish to find out are:

- The order of grapheme–phoneme correspondences in the programme.
- How grapheme–phoneme correspondences are taught.
- Are there associated decodable texts?
- Is training available?
- Are there in-built assessments?
- What resources and teaching aids are available?
- Are electronic resources available?
- Is it possible to observe someone teaching using the programme?

What to do next?

Reinforce your knowledge of different programmes by:

- Observing lessons in schools.

- Looking at resources for different programmes.

- Discussing different programmes with teachers.

- Looking at websites for different programmes.

- Find out more about THRASS (see 'Recommended reading' below).

Websites

There are several useful websites, including:

Debbie Hepplewhite's SyntheticPhonics.com (**http://syntheticphonics.com/**).

Reading by Six: how the best schools do it (**http://www.ofsted.gov.uk/resources/ reading-six-how-best-schools-do-it**).

Recommended reading

Davies, A. and Ritchie, D. (1998) *THRASS: teacher's manual*. Chester: THRASS (UK) (for guidance on the principles and practice for THRASS (Teaching Handwriting Reading and Spelling Skills)).

DCSF (2007) *Letters and Sounds: principles and practice of high quality phonics: notes of guidance for practitioners and teachers*. London: DfES.

DfE (2011) *Criteria for Assuring High-quality Phonic Work*. Runcorn: DfE (available at **www.education.gov.uk/schools/teachingandlearning/pedagogy/phonics/ a0010240/criteria-forassuring-high-quality-phonic-work**).

Jolliffe, W. and Waugh, D. with Carss, A. (2012) *Teaching Systematic Synthetic Phonics in Primary Schools*. London: Learning Matters/SAGE (Chapter 13).

jollylearning.co.uk/overview-about-jolly-phonics/ (for guidance on the principles and practice for Jolly Phonics).

Ofsted (2010) *Reading by Six: how the best schools do it*. London: Ofsted.

Read Write Inc. (2011) *Phonics Handbook*. Oxford: Oxford University Press (for guidance on the principles and practice for Read Write Inc.).

ruthmiskinliteracy.com (for guidance on the principles and practice for Read Write Inc.).

thrass.co.uk (for guidance on the principles and practice for THRASS (Teaching Handwriting Reading and Spelling Skills)).

Conclusion

Now that you have worked through the chapters, you should be ready to attempt the longer audit in Appendix 2. If you are still a little unsure about any aspects of systematic synthetic phonics, go back to the relevant chapters and look at the audits and answers again. Look, too, at Jolliffe *et al*. (2012) where you will find more details about each aspect.

Some of the terminology may confuse you, but you will soon become familiar with terms and their meaning as you gain more experience of planning and teaching phonics. The most important thing is that you develop your teaching skills and your understanding of how to plan a systematic programme of lessons and activities for the children you teach. If this is underpinned by a sound understanding of systematic synthetic phonics, you will be on your way to becoming an outstanding teacher of reading.

David Waugh

Ruth Harrison-Palmer

August 2013

Appendix 1

Initial audit answers

What does word recognition refer to in the Simple View of Reading?
*The ability to master the **alphabetic code**, apply phonic knowledge and skills in order to decode words and develop a store of familiar **tricky word**s.*
What does language comprehension refer to in the Simple View of Reading?
Processes by which texts, as well as spoken language, are understood and interpreted.
What is a phoneme?
A phoneme is the smallest unit of sound in a word that can change its meaning.
What is a grapheme?
A grapheme is a symbol of a phoneme – that is, a letter or group of letters representing a sound.
How many phonemes do you think there are in English?
It is generally agreed that there are 44 phonemes in spoken English, although some phonics programmes use 43 or 45.
What is blending?
Drawing individual sounds together to pronounce a word, e.g. /c/l/a/p/ blended together reads clap.
What is segmenting?
Splitting up a word into its individual phonemes in order to spell it – i.e. the word pat *has three phonemes: /p/a/t/.*
How many vowel sounds do you think there are?
There are 20 vowel sounds in English.
How many consonant sounds?
There are 24 consonant sounds in English.
What is encoding?
The process of translating sounds into letters to spell words.
What is decoding?
*The process of deciphering letters in order to read words by translating **graphemes** into sounds.*

The number of phonemes in words:	
cat	3 /c/a/t/
book	3 /b/oo/k/
flat	4 /f/l/a/t/
splash	5 /s/p/l/a/sh/
crack	4 /c/r/a/ck/
blend	5 /b/l/e/n/d/
phonics	6 /ph/o/n/i/c/s/

Appendix 2

Long audit

Discriminating sounds and phonemes

Match the terms below to their definitions:

1. phonemes

2. graphemes

3. phonological awareness

4. phonemic awareness

5. adjacent consonants

A. This involves being able to hear, recall and manipulate sounds.

B. These are individual sounds. In English, there are around 44 (the number varies slightly according to accent and which phonics programme you look at).

C. The ability to hear and manipulate the phonemes in spoken words and to remember the order of phonemes in words. For example, the phonemes in the word *big* can be segmented as /b/ /i/ /g/.

D. Consonants which are side by side but have separate phonemes, for example, s/t in *stop*, c/l in *club* and s/t/r in *strip*. Although we blend these sounds together, it is important to emphasise that the letters each have individual sounds.

E. These are phonemes written down, so in the word *cat* there are three phonemes and they are represented by three graphemes /c/a/t/. In the word *shop* there are three phonemes but the first is represented by two letters making one sound (a digraph): /sh/o/p/.

Segmenting words

Look at the words below and count the phonemes for each and then split the word into phonemes. The first one has been done for you:

Word	Number of phonemes	Split the word into phonemes	Word	Number of phonemes	Split the word into phonemes
when	3	/wh/e/n/	straw		
leg			flash		
blast			splinter		
save			bride		

Segmenting using a phoneme frame

Use the frame below to segment the following words: *flood, crush, scratch, shoe, shampoo.* The first one has been done for you:

f	l	oo	d		

Some challenges when teaching and learning phonics

Match the terms below to their definitions:

1. accent

2. dialect

3. schwa

4. enunciation

5. grapheme variation

6. phoneme variation

A. This means to pronounce or articulate. It is important that we sound phonemes clearly and accurately when teaching children. This means avoiding adding additional sounds such as the schwa wherever possible. For many letters this is quite easy – for example, f, l, m, n, r, s. For some, however, it is difficult to avoid (b, d, t), but you should try to keep this as short as possible.

B. This is the way we pronounce words, whereas our dialect has a grammatical structure, even if this is not written down as with Standard English.

C. Many phonemes can be represented by different graphemes. For example, the *ie* sound in *tie* can be represented by *-igh* in *high*, *y* in *by* and *eigh* in *height*.

D. These vary from place to place and include words, phrases and clauses which may not appear in other areas. Standard English is often accepted as 'correct' and is the version in which English should be written. It should not be confused with accent.

E. Many graphemes can represent different phonemes. For example, *g* has different sounds in *gate*, *germ* and *regime*.

F. This is a short vowel sound such as we hear in words like *above*, *about*, *the*, *pencil*, *doctor* and *taken*. The symbol often used for this sound in dictionaries is ə.

A phonic problem

A child in your Year 1 class often writes 'words' with no vowels, for example *bt* for *butter*, *cl* for *colour*:

- Why you think the problem arose?
- How you might address it?

Grapheme variations

Many phonemes can be represented by more than one grapheme – for example, the /sh/ sound in *shop* can be *ch* in *chef*, *s* in *sugar* and *ci* in *suspicious*. How many ways can you represent each of the following?

- the /e/ sound in bed
- the /s/ sound in sock
- the /oa/ sound in boat

Phoneme variations

Look at the graphemes below and see how many alternative phonemes each can be used to represent, providing a word for each example. The first one has been done for you:

- *g* – go, giant, gnaw, regime
- *o*
- *ough*
- *ch*

Grapheme–phoneme correspondences and 'tricky' words

Match the definitions with the terms:

1. The spelling system of a language – i.e. the ways in which graphemes and phonemes relate to each other. The English orthographic system is more complex than many languages, since most phonemes can be represented by more than one grapheme.

2. Words which can be easily decoded using phonic strategies – e.g. *cat*, *dog*, *lamp*.

3. The act of translating graphemes into phonemes – i.e. reading.

4. The act of transcribing units of sound or phonemes into graphemes – i.e. spelling.

5. Words that are not easily decoded because they do not conform to common grapheme–phoneme correspondences.

6. A device for remembering something, such as 'ee/ee/ feel the tree'.

7. For some words which have tricky parts such as silent letters, we remember how to spell them by sounding the silent or less pronounced phonemes. For example, we remember how to spell Wednesday by saying Wed-nes-day.

A. phonically irregular

B. orthographic system

C. decoding

D. over-syllabification

E. encoding

F. mnemonic

G. decodable

Identifying the tricky bits in some common English words

Identify the tricky bits of the words below and state why this part presents problems for readers and writers. This will be the part which readers may find difficult or irregular. The first one has been done for you and is presented in bold type and underlined:

- h**ea**d (because *ea* is more often sounded as in *beat* and *meat*)

- knot

- women

- sure

- write

- who

Decoding and encoding text

Match the terms below to their definitions:

1. segmenting

2. blending

3. synthetic phonics

4. decodable texts

A. This involves separating words into phonemes and then blending the phonemes together to read the word. This compares with analytic phonics in which segments or parts of words are analysed and patterns are compared with other words.

B. Texts which can be easily decoded using phonic strategies available to children at a particular stage in a phonics programme – e.g. *cat*, *dog*, *lamp*.

C. Splitting up a word into its individual phonemes in order to spell it – i.e. the word *pat* has three phonemes: /p/a/t/.

D. To draw individual sounds together to pronounce a word – e.g. /c/l/a/p/ blended together reads *clap*.

Vowel digraphs

Look at the terms below and provide a definition and a word for each, underling the relevant grapheme. The first one has been done for you:

- split digraph – n<u>ose</u>

- quadgraph

- vowel digraph

- long vowel phoneme

- short vowel phoneme

- trigraph

Look at the words below and sort them into those with short vowel digraphs and those with long vowel digraphs:

rough, like, meet, weird, show, head, break, said, cough

Short vowel digraphs	Long vowel digraphs

Now look at the words below and identify those which include split vowel digraphs:

fine, street, spoke, rose, refine, take, straight, slope

Sort the words below into the correct columns based on the long vowel phoneme each contains. This may be represented by a number of different graphemes. There are some examples, already in the table, to help you:

boy, me, fl<u>oa</u>t, l<u>ime</u>, h<u>ow</u>, lady, th<u>ough</u>, she, sn<u>ow</u>, m<u>ake</u>, str<u>ay</u>, sp<u>oi</u>l, m<u>ea</u>t, t<u>ie</u>, dr<u>ough</u>t, st<u>oa</u>t, th<u>ey</u>, br<u>ea</u>k, ann<u>oy</u>, t<u>ow</u>n, w<u>eigh</u>t, t<u>igh</u>t, m<u>ea</u>l, thr<u>one</u>, del<u>ete</u>, tr<u>y</u>, al<u>ou</u>d, h<u>eigh</u>t, b<u>one</u>

/ee/	/ie/	/oe/	/ae/	/ow/	/oi/
r<u>ee</u>l	t<u>i</u>me	st<u>one</u>	st<u>ay</u>	n<u>ow</u>	<u>oi</u>ntment
sp<u>ea</u>k	f<u>i</u>nd	sh<u>ow</u>	dr<u>ai</u>n	pr<u>ou</u>d	t<u>oy</u>

Spelling

Match the terms to their definitions:

1. plural

2. medial vowel sound

3. homographs

4. prefix

5. homonyms

6. homophones

7. morpheme

8. singular

9. compound word

10. suffix

A. A word form used to refer to one of something.

B. Words which refer to more than one item. This usually involves adding an *s* (cats, books) or *es* (matches, buses), but some are irregular. For example, child becomes children, mouse becomes mice, and goose becomes geese. Some nouns remain the same in their plural form as in their singular form, including sheep and the names of many fish (one haddock, two haddock, one salmon, two salmon).

C. The smallest unit of language that can convey meaning.

D. Morphemes which are placed at the beginning of a word to modify or change its meaning – for example, dis/like, micro/scope, tri/cycle.

E. Morphemes added to the ends of words to modify their meanings – for example, use and useful or useless; look and looking, looks or looked.

F. Words with the same spelling and pronunciation but different meanings – for example, left (opposite of right) and left (departed), bark (of a dog) and bark (of a tree).

G. Words which sound the same but have different spellings and meanings – for example, sea and see, sew, so and sow, blue and blew, great and grate. The word means 'same sound'.

H. Words which are spelled the same as other words which mean something different and are pronounced differently – for example, sow (spreading seeds) and sow (a female pig); lead (to take charge or something used to restrain a dog) and lead (a heavy metal); row (argue) and row (in a boat). The word means 'same writing'.

I. A word made when two words are joined to form a new word – for example, toothbrush, football, toenail. Hyphens are sometimes used to link the two parts of the word – for example, twenty-seven, self-audit, penalty-taker.

J. The sound of the phoneme in the middle of a word, so that hot and cot have the same medial vowel sound.

Sorting words according to medial vowel sound

Sort the words below into groups according to their medial vowel sound:

bat, dig, bun, tag, frog, when, cut, man, sock, grim, sat, but, fun, pin, bet, web

Modifying words

Look at the words below and see how many new words you can create from them by adding morphemes – for example, *discover* could become *rediscover, discovery, discovers, discovered*:

- position
- possess
- produce

Compound words

Look at the compound words below and separate them into the words which are put together to create them. The first one has been done for you:

- *someone*   *some + one*
- *toothpaste*
- *handwrite*
- *headteacher*
- *mastermind*
- *bookshelf*

Spelling rules and generalisations

Describe a spelling rule or spelling generalisation for making words which end with *y* into plurals. The singulars and plurals below should help you:

- *baby – babies*
- *pony – ponies*
- *key – keys*
- *day – days*
- *monkey – monkeys*

The spelling rule 'I before e except after c' is often said to be flawed. Why is this? What could you add to the mnemonic 'I before e except after c' to make it into a more reliable rule?

Phonics in the early years

Match the terms to their definitions:

A. general sound discrimination

B. quality first teaching

C. oral segmenting and blending

D. language-rich curriculum

E. voice sounds

F. alliteration

G. phonological awareness

1. A curriculum that has speaking and listening at its centre. Links are made between language and practical experiences. It provides an environment rich in print and provides many opportunities to engage with books.

2. This includes a blend of whole-class, group and individual activities designed to match work to children's different but developing abilities.

3. The ability to attend to the phonological or sound structure of language as distinct from its meaning.

4. Blending and segmenting words without using knowledge of grapheme–phoneme correspondence – i.e. without showing written forms.

5. The process of allowing children to become attuned to the sounds around them.

6. A sequence of words beginning with the same sound – for example, 'seven silly sailors sat upon a seat'.

7. In early stages of phonological development children engage in activities to help them distinguish between different vocal sounds. This might include oral blending and segmenting.

Aspects of phonological awareness

Phase 1 in *Letters and Sounds* includes a range of activities, designed to develop phonological awareness, that are separated into seven aspects:

- Aspect 1: general sound discrimination – environmental sounds.

- Aspect 2: general sound discrimination – instrumental sounds.

- Aspect 3: general sound discrimination – body percussion.

- Aspect 4: rhythm and rhyme.

- Aspect 5: alliteration.

- Aspect 6: voice sounds.

- Aspect 7: oral blending and segmenting.

Read the description of the activity below, taken from phase 1 in *Letters and Sounds*, and decide which aspect of phonological awareness above it is designed to teach:

Making trumpets
Make amplifiers (trumpet shapes) from simple cones of paper or lightweight card, and experiment, by making different noises through the cones. Model sounds for the children: the up and down wail of a siren, the honk of a fog horn, a peep, peep, peep of a bird. Contrast loud and soft sounds. Invite the children to share their favourite sound for the rest of the group to copy. Use the trumpets to sound out phonemes that begin each child's name.

Multisensory approaches

Match the terms with their definitions:

1. multisensory classroom environment

2. kinaesthetic

3. interactive approaches to phonics

4. visual

5. auditory

A. Activities which encourage children to look at different resources, graphemes etc.

B. Approaches to phonics involve activities which encourage children to listen to different resources, phonemes etc.

C. Some people learn better using some form of physical activity: hence the use of actions to accompany phonemes and graphemes in Jolly Phonics.

D. A classroom in which children can use all of a range of senses (hearing, seeing, feeling, moving).

E. This ensures that children are actively involved in their learning and take a full part in lessons.

Teaching a systematic and structured programme

Provide an explanation for each of the following:

- fidelity to a programme
- systematic progression
- criteria for assuring high-quality phonic work

Planning for phonics

Name the four elements of a well-structured phonics lesson.

Assessment

What are the two processes involved in the Simple View of Reading? Provide an explanation of each of the processes.

Match the terms to their definitions:

A. word recognition

B. language comprehension

C. diagnostic assessment

D. tracking pupil progress

E. pseudo-words

F. formative assessment

1. This forms an integral part of teaching and learning. It contributes to learning through providing feedback and should inform future planning and next steps.

2. This assesses the nature of difficulties that a child might have.

3. This involves using assessments to identify children who may need additional support. It is also used to inform the organisation of phonic work. It is designed to make sure all children make maximum progress.

4. These are nonsense words which are used to assess children's ability to decode.

5. The ability to read the words on the page.

6. The ability to understand oral and written language.

Phonics at Key Stage 2

Match the terms with their definitions:

1. free morpheme

2. etymology

3. monosyllabic words

4. bound morpheme

5. adjacent consonants

6. grapheme–phoneme correspondence

A. The origins of the formation of a word and its meaning.

B. The relationship between letters and sounds. The graphemes (letters and combinations of letters such as digraphs and trigraphs) are the written representation on the phonemes (sounds) in words.

C. Consonants which appear next to each other in a word and can be blended together – e.g. *bl* in *blip*, *cr* in *crack* (note that the *ck* in *crack* is a digraph, as the consonants come together to form a single sound or phoneme).

D. Words with one syllable – for example, *book*, *dig*, *run*, *hot*.

E. A morpheme which can stand alone as a word – for example, in *kicked*, *kick* is a free morpheme, but *-ed* is a bound morpheme because it cannot stand alone – it needs to be bound to a word to have meaning.

F. A morpheme which cannot stand alone (see free morpheme).

Meanings of morphemes

Look at the list of prefixes below and the words next to them and provide a definition for each prefix:

- *dis-*   *dislike*

- *tri-*   *tricycle*

- *pre-*   *predated*
- *un-*   *unusual*
- *post-*   *postnatal*

Different phonics programmes and resources

Which programme is being described? Choose from Letters and Sounds, Read Write Inc., Phonics Bug, Jolly Phonics (one appears twice):

1. It has a chart of speed sounds.

2. There are six phases, the first of which only involves oral work.

3. It is based upon *Letters and Sounds* and has a range of books, some of which can be used interactively for teaching.

4. There are actions for each phoneme.

5. There is a mnemonic to go with each grapheme–phoneme correspondence – for example *Maisie's Mountain* and *poo at the zoo*, *cup of tea for ea*, *what can you see?* (for *ee*).

Appendix 3

Long audit answers

Discriminating sounds and phonemes

You were asked to match the terms to their definitions. Answers: 1B, 2E, 3A, 4C, 5D.

Segmenting words

You were asked to look at the words below and count the phonemes for each and then split the word into phonemes. Answers:

Word	Number of phonemes	Split the word into phonemes	Word	Number of phonemes	Split the word into phonemes
when	3	/wh/e/n/	straw	4	/s/t/r/aw
leg	3	/l/e/g/	flash	4	/f/l/a/sh
blast	5	/b/l/a/s/t/	splinter	7	/s/p/l/i/n/t/er
save	3	/s/ae/v	bride	4	/b/r/ie/d

Segmenting using a phoneme frame

You were asked to use the frame below to segment the following words: *flood*, *crush*, *scratch*, *shoe*, *shampoo*. Answers:

f	l	oo	d		
c	r	u	sh		
s	c	r	a	tch	
sh	oe				
sh	a	m	p	oo	

Some challenges when teaching and learning phonics

You were asked to match the terms to their definitions. Answers: 1B, 2D, 3F, 4A, 5C, 6E.

A phonic problem

A child in your Year 1 class often writes 'words' with no vowels – for example, *bt* for *butter*, *cl* for *colour*.

Why you think the problem arose?

This may be due to the child being taught phonics by someone who did not enunciate 'cleanly', adding a schwa sound when sounding phonemes – for example, 'fuh', 'luh' and 'muh' instead of the correct 'fff', 'lll' and 'mmm'. The child has, therefore, assumed that *buh* and *tuh* are all that are needed to make the word *butter*, and *cuh* and *luh* are all that are needed to make *colour*.

How you might address it

It is important to handle this carefully, especially if the person who has 'helped' the child is a parent or carer. You may wish to invite parents and carers to help in the classroom where you can model enunciation, or you might organise a workshop for parents to provide guidance on ways of helping their children with reading.

Take care to enunciate the phonemes as 'cleanly' as possible when working with the children (this is easy for many letters, but it is difficult to avoid adding a slight vowel sound to letters such as b, c, d and p). Talk with children about why it is important to enunciate well and practise with them. Make use of resources such as Sonic Phonics, which have electronic devices which enunciate correctly, and use websites which provide good models, such as Mr Thorne Does Phonics (**http://www.youtube.com/watch?v=hm4nhA4b-2Q**).

Grapheme variations

You were asked to see how many ways you can represent the sounds in each of the words below. Possible answers include:

- the /e/ sound in *bed* – *head*, *said*

- the /s/ sound in *sock* – *city*, *glass*, *dance*, *suspense*

- the /oa/ sound in *boat* – *stone*, *know*, *toe*, *go*, *though*

Phoneme variations

You were asked to look at the graphemes below and see how many alternative phonemes each can be used to represent, providing a word for each example. Possible answers include:

- *g* – *go*, *giant*, *gnaw*, *regime*

- *o* – *on*, *go*, *do*, *to*, *woman*, *women*

- *ough* – *tough*, *cough*, *bough*, *though*, *ought*, *through*, *hiccough*, *thorough*

- *ch* – *chip*, *chef*, *school*

Grapheme–phoneme correspondences and 'tricky' words

You were asked to match the terms to their definitions. Answers: 1B, 2G, 3C, 4E, 5A, 6F, 7D.

Identifying the tricky bits in some common English words

You were asked to identify the tricky bits of the words below and state why this part presents problems for readers and writers. Possible answers:

- h<u>ea</u>d (because *ea* is more often sounded as in *beat* and *meat*)
- <u>kn</u>ot (because the *k* is silent)
- w<u>om</u><u>e</u>n (because the *o* and *e* are pronounced as /i/ in *pin*)
- <u>s</u>ure (because *s* is pronounced like the /sh/ in ship)
- <u>wr</u>ite (because a more common representation of the sound would be /r/)
- <u>who</u> (because the *wh* is sounded like the /h/ in hoot, and the *o* is sounded like the *oo* in boot)

Decoding and encoding text

You were asked to match the terms to their definitions. Answers: 1C, 2D, 3A, 4B.

Vowel digraphs

You were asked to look at the terms below and provide a definition and a word for each, underling the relevant grapheme. The first one was done for you. Answers could include:

1. Split digraph – two letters, making one sound, but separated by a consonant, e.g. a-e as in c<u>ake</u>, n<u>ose</u>.
2. Quadgraph – four letters which combine to make a new sound, e.g. th<u>ough</u>t, <u>eigh</u>t.
3. Vowel digraph – two letters that are combined to produce a long or a short vowel phoneme, for example, <u>ea</u>t, kn<u>ow</u>, h<u>ea</u>d (note that vowel digraphs can include consonants).w
4. Long vowel phoneme – the long vowel sounds as in f<u>ee</u>l or c<u>o</u>ld, afr<u>ai</u>d, ab<u>ou</u>t.
5. Short vowel phoneme – the short vowel sounds as in h<u>a</u>t or s<u>ai</u>d, s<u>a</u>d, h<u>ea</u>d.
6. Trigraph – three letters which combine to make a new sound, e.g. h<u>air</u>, h<u>igh</u>.

You were asked to look at the words below and sort them into those with short vowel digraphs and those with long vowel digraphs:

rough, like, meet, weird, show, head, break, said, cough

Answers:

short vowel digraphs	long vowel digraphs
rough, cough, said, head	break, like, meet, weird, show

You were asked to look at the words below and identify those which include split vowel digraphs. Answers:

- *fine, spoke, rose, refine, take, straight, slope*
- *street* has a long vowel digraph /ee/, but it is not split
- *straight* has a long vowel quadgraph, /aigh/

You were asked to sort the words below into the correct columns based on the long vowel phoneme each contains. This may be represented by a number of different graphemes:

boy, me, float, lime, how, lady, though, she, snow, make, stray, spoil, meat, tie, drought, stoat, they, break, annoy, town, weight, tight, meal, throne, delete, try, aloud, height, bone

Answers (the first two in each column were examples):

/ee/	/ie/	/oe/	/ae/	/ow/	/oi/
reel	time	stone	stay	now	ointment
speak	find	show	drain	proud	toy
me	lime	float	lady	how	boy
she	tie	though	make	drought	spoil
meat	tight	snow	stray	town	annoy
meal	try	stoat	they		aloud
delete	height	throne	break		
		bone	weight		

Spelling

You were asked to match the terms to their definitions. Answers: 1B, 2J, 3H, 4D, 5F, 6G, 7C, 8A, 9I, 10E.

Sorting words according to medial vowel sound

Sort the words below into groups according to their medial vowel sound:

bat, dig, bun, tag, frog, when, cut, man, sock, grim, sat, but, fun, pin, bet, web

Answers:

- *bat, tag, man, sat*
- *bet, web, when*
- *but, fun, bun, cut*
- *frog, sock*
- *dig, grim, pin*

Modifying words

You were asked to look at the words below and see how many new words you could create from them by adding morphemes. For example, *discover* could become *rediscover, discovery, discovers, discovered, discoverer*. Possible answers include:

- **position** – *disposition, reposition, positioned, positions, positional, positionally, proposition, reposition, positioner*
- **possess** – *dispossess, repossess, possesses, possessed, possessing, prepossess, possession, possessions, prepossessing, unprepossessing*
- **produce** – *producer, produces, produced, producing, producers, product, reproduce, reproduction, production, productivity, productive*

Compound words

You were asked to look at the compound words below and separate them into the words which are put together to create them. Answers:

- *toothpaste*   *tooth + paste*
- *handwrite*   *hand + write*
- *headteacher*   *head + teacher*
- *mastermind*   *master + mind*
- *bookshelf*   *book + shelf*

Spelling rules and generalisations

You were asked to describe a spelling rule or spelling generalisation for making words which end with *y* into plurals. You were given the following examples to help you:

- *baby – babies*
- *pony – ponies*

- *key – keys*

- *day – days*

- *monkey – monkeys*

Answer:

Rule/generalisation: if the singular has a vowel before the final *y*, add *s* to make it plural – e.g. *boy – boys*. If the singular has a consonant before the final *y*, remove the *y* and add *-ies*. (This almost always works and exceptions are very rare.)

You were asked to look at the spelling rule 'I before e except after c', which is often said to be flawed, and to explain why this is and how the rule could be improved.

There are many exceptions to the rule, including in very common words such as their, being, seeing, rein, reign, height, weight and weird. What could you add to the mnemonic 'I before e except after c' to make it into a more reliable rule? There would still be exceptions, but if you added 'when the word rhymes with me', the rule would be more reliable.

NB Some people use the phrase 'the exception that proves the rule' to suggest that exceptions actually prove or demonstrate that a rule works. Actually, 'prove' comes from the Latin *probare* – to test – and this is how it was used when the phrase originated, so exceptions test the rule and in this case it possibly fails the test!

Phonics in the early years

You were asked to match the terms to their definitions. Answers: A5, B2, C4, D1, E5, F6, G3.

Aspects of phonological awareness

You were asked read the description of the activity below, taken from phase 1 in *Letters and Sounds*, and decide which aspect of phonological awareness above it is designed to teach.

Making trumpets
Make amplifiers (trumpet shapes) from simple cones of paper or lightweight card and experiment, by making different noises through the cones. Model sounds for the children: the up and down wail of a siren, the honk of a fog horn, a peep, peep, peep of a bird. Contrast loud and soft sounds. Invite the children to share their favourite sound for the rest of the group to copy. Use the trumpets to sound out phonemes that begin with each child's name.

Answer: making trumpets is designed to teach Aspect 6: voice sounds. It allows children to 'tune into' sounds and to distinguish between different vocal sounds.

Multisensory approaches

You were asked to match the terms to their definitions. Answers: 1D, 2C, 3E, 4A, 5B.

Teaching a systematic and structured programme

You were asked to provide an explanation for each of the following:

- fidelity to a programme

- systematic progression

- criteria for assuring high-quality phonic work

Possible answers:

Fidelity to a programme
When teaching systematic, synthetic phonics, it is important to adhere to a teaching framework that ensures that all grapheme–phoneme correspondences are taught. This does not necessarily mean that only one programme can be used. However, mixing too many elements from different programmes can result in a lack of essential coherence across a teaching framework.

Systematic progression
An effective systematic, synthetic phonics programme begins with learning grapheme–phoneme correspondences (GPCs) in a specific order. These are used to blend CVC words from the outset. Following on from that, more GPCs are taught until all 40+ phonemes are introduced. Some 'tricky words', that are complex to decode, are introduced at a pace of approx. 3–5 per week. Next, alternative pronunciations and spellings for graphemes are taught. Application of GPCs taught in reading and writing is provided throughout.

Criteria for assuring high-quality phonic work
The DfE provides schools with criteria which define the key features of an effective, systematic, synthetic phonics programme. Published programmes should meet each of the criteria. These can be accessed at **http://www.education.gov.uk/schools/teachingandlearning/ pedagogy/a0010240/criteria-for-assuring-high-quality-phonic-work**.

Planning for phonics

You were asked to name the four elements of a well-structured phonics lesson:

- revisit/review

- teach

- practise

- apply

Assessment

You were asked about the two processes involved in the Simple View of Reading and were asked to provide an explanation of each of the processes.

Possible answers:

- word recognition processes and language comprehension processes

- word recognition processes involve the ability to read the words on the page

- language comprehension processes encompass the ability to understand oral and written language

You were asked to match the terms to their definitions. Answers: A5, B6, C2, D3, E4, F1.

Phonics at Key Stage 2

You were asked to match the terms to their definitions. Answers: 1E, 2A, 3D, 4F, 5C, 6B.

Meanings of morphemes

You were asked to look at the list of prefixes below and the words next to them and provide a definition for each prefix:

- *dis-*   *dislike*

- *tri-*   *tricycle*

- *pre-*   *predated*

- *un-*   *unusual*

- *post-*   *postnatal*

Different phonics programmes and resources

You were asked which programme was being described for each of the statements below. You could choose from Letters and Sounds, Read Write Inc., Phonics Bug, Jolly Phonics (one appears twice).

Answers:

- It has a chart of speed sounds (Read Write Inc.).

- There are six phases, the first of which only involves oral work (Letters and Sounds).

- It is based upon Letters and Sounds and has a range of books, some of which can be used interactively for teaching (Phonics Bug).

- There are actions for each phoneme (Jolly Phonics).

- There is a mnemonic to go with each grapheme–phoneme correspondence – for example, *Maisie's Mountain* and *poo at the zoo*, *cup of tea for ea*, *what can you see?* (for *ee*) (Read Write Inc.).

Index

accents 8
adjacent consonants 3, 82
alliteration 42
alternative spellings 15, 17
analytic phonics 22
assessment 65–77, 109–10, 119
auditory 46, 48

blending 3, 22, 42, 47
bound morphemes 79, 82

challenges 6–11, 101–2, 112–13
classroom environment, multisensory 46
compound words 31–2, 33, 35–6, 106, 116
consonant digraphs 47
consonants, adjacent 3, 82
core criteria 92
criteria
    for high quality phonic work 50–1, 56
    for successful programmes 92

decodable 16
decodable sentences 20–1
decodable texts 22, 91
decoding 16, 19–24, 103–4, 114
diagnostic assessment 71
dialects 8
digraphs *see* consonant digraphs; vowel
    digraphs
discrete daily sessions 91
discrete teaching of phonics 43

early years phonics 39–44, 107–8, 117–18
encoding 16, 19–24, 103–4, 114
enunciation 8–9
etymology 81

fidelity to a framework/structure 55, 91
Floppy's Phonics 89
formative assessment 71
free morphemes 79, 82

general sound discrimination 42
grammatical awareness 21
grapheme variations 7, 9, 10, 102, 113
grapheme-phoneme correspondences 13–18, 55,
    82, 102–3, 114
graphemes 3
grotty graphemes 13–14, 16–17

homographs 32, 33, 36
homonyms 32, 33, 36
homophones 32, 33, 36

I spy 40–1
Independent Review of the Teaching
    of Early Reading 39–40, 42–3
interactive approaches 47

Jolliffe, W. 59
Jolly Phonics 46, 89

Key Stage 2, phonics at 78–88, 101–11, 119
kinaesthetic 46, 48

language comprehension 71
language-rich curriculum 41, 42
lesson plan 60–1, 62–3
Letters and Sounds 9, 14, 21, 40, 51, 67, 90, 91, 108
listening 42
long vowel digraphs 25–9, 104–5, 114–15
long vowel phoneme charts 26, 28
long vowel phonemes 26, 27

medial vowel sound 34
    sorting words according to 30–1, 34, 106, 115–16
mnemonics 16
monosyllabic words 82
morphemes 33
    bound 79, 82
    exploring 78–9, 82
    free 79, 82
    meanings of 79, 82–3, 110–11, 119
    segmenting words into 79, 83
multisensory approaches 45–9, 108–9, 118

Ofsted 90, 92
oral segmenting *see* segmentation
orthographic system 15

pace 51, 57
phases 92
phoneme charts, long vowel 26, 28
phoneme frames 2, 99, 112
phoneme variations 7–8, 9, 10–11, 102, 113
phonemes 2
    discriminating sounds and 1–5, 100–1, 112
    lesson to developing blending 47
    see also grapheme-phoneme correspondences

phonemic awareness 3
phonemic frames 4
phonic knowledge
    for reading/decoding 19–21, 22
    for spelling/encoding 21, 23
phonically irregular 16
phonics
    at Key Stage 2 78–88, 110–11, 119
    challenges/problems 6–11, 101–2, 112–13
    decoding and encoding text 19–24, 103–4, 114
    discriminating sounds and phonemes 1–5,
        100–1, 112
    grapheme-phoneme correspondences
        and tricky words 13–18, 102–3, 114
    long vowel digraphs 25–9, 104–5, 114–15
    multisensory approaches 45–9, 108–9, 118
    planning for 59–63, 109, 118
    spelling 30–8, 105–6, 115–16
    teaching in the early years 39–44, 107–8,
        117–18
    teaching a systematic and structured
        programmes 50–8, 109, 118
    tracking and assessment 65–77, 109–10, 119
    using a range of programmes and
        resources 89–95, 111, 119–20
Phonics Bug 90
phonics first and fast 91
phonological awareness 3, 40–1, 42, 43, 108,
    117–18
planning for phonics 59–63, 109, 118
play, power of 41, 43
plural 33
poetry 81, 85–6
prefixes 33, 78–9, 82
programme quiz 90–1, 93–4
programmes and resources 89–95, 111, 119–20
    see also systematic structured programmes
progress checks 67, 75
progression 51, 55–6, 57
pseudo-words 71

quadgraphs 27
quality first teaching 42, 42–3
quality phonic work, criteria for assuring 50–1, 56

Read Write Inc 13, 16, 90
reading *see* decoding
Reading by Six (Ofsted) 90, 92
resources *see* programmes and resources
rhymes 81, 85–6
Rose Review 39–40, 42–3

schwa 8
screening checks 67–71, 75–6
segmentation 1–2, 3–4, 22, 42, 79, 83,
    100–1, 112
sentences, composing decodable 20–1
short vowel phonemes 25, 26, 27
Simple View of Reading 65–6, 71–5
singular 32
sound discrimination, general 42
sounds, discriminating phonemes
    and 1–5, 100–1, 112
Sounds Write 90
speaking 42
spelling 30–8, 105–7, 115–17
    application of phonic knowledge 21, 23
    exploring alternative 15, 17
    rules and generalisations 32, 36–7, 107,
        116–17
spelling list (Year 3-4), identifying vowel
    digraphs in 26, 27–8
split vowel digraphs 5, 26, 27, 47–8
Standard English 8
story sounds 40
suffixes 33, 78, 79, 82, 83
synthetic phonics 22
systematic structured
    programmes 50–8, 109, 118
    see also programmes and resources

teaching sequence 59, 60–1, 61, 62–3
text, decoding and encoding 19–24,
    103–4, 114
tracking and assessment 65–77, 109–10, 119
tricky words 13–18, 102–3, 114
trigraphs 27

visual 46, 48
voice sounds 42
vowel digraphs, long 25–9, 104–5, 114–15

word recognition 71
words
    identifying tricky 14–15, 17, 103
    modifying 31, 34–5, 80–1, 83–5,
        106, 116
    playing with 41
    segmenting *see* segmentation
    sorting according to medial
        vowel sound 30–1, 34, 106, 115–16
    see also compound words; monosyllabic
        words; pseudo-words